W9-ACB-921

IN MEMORY OF:

Lois Jean Davies

PRESENTED BY:

Jill Amweg
Susan Burchfield
Jules Krizan

TIMBER PRESS
POCKET GUIDE TO
Clematis

TIMBER PRESS
POCKET GUIDE TO

Clematis

MARY TOOMEY
with Everett Leeds
and
Charles Chesshire

635.93
TOO

TIMBER PRESS

Frontispiece: *Clematis* 'Jackmanii'. Photo by M. Toomey.

Copyright © 2006 by Mary Toomey, Everett Leeds, and Charles Chesshire. All rights reserved.

Published in 2006 by

Timber Press, Inc.
The Haseltine Building
133 S.W. Second Avenue, Suite 450
Portland, Oregon 97204-3527, U.S.A.

www.timberpress.com

For contact information regarding editorial, marketing, sales, and distribution in the United Kingdom, see www.timberpress.co.uk.

Printed through Colorcraft Ltd., Hong Kong

Toomey, Mary.
   Timber Press pocket guide to clematis / Mary Toomey, with Everett Leeds and Charles Chesshire.
      p. cm.
   Includes bibliographical references and index.
   ISBN-13: 978-0-88192-814-3
   ISBN-10: 0-88192-814-3
   1. Clematis. I. Leeds, Everett. II. Chesshire, Charles. III. Timber Press (Portland, Or.) IV. Title. V. Title: Pocket guide to clematis.
   SB413.C6T67 2006
   635.9'3334--dc22
                                    2006009779

A catalog record for this book is also available from the British Library.

Dedication

To our parents

Acknowledgments

Thanks again to all those people and places mentioned in *An Illustrated Encyclopedia of Clematis*, on which this pocket guide is based. Special thanks to Raymond J. Evison, Szczepan Marczyński, and the Ozawa Slide Library of Japan for contributing photographs to this guide.

About This Book

The plant descriptions in this book are arranged in alphabetical order by scientific name and in accordance with the *International Clematis Register and Checklist*, first published in 2002. Cultivar names are enclosed in single quote marks. Trade names (selling names) are not. For example, the cultivar *Clematis* 'Kugotia', which has a trade name, is listed as *C.* 'Kugotia' (Golden Tiara), and *C.* 'Kacper', which has a translated name in the trade, is listed as *C.* 'Kacper' (Caspar). Some synonyms are included as are either translations of selected foreign names or their meanings. The name in its original language is the correct cultivar name. Where the species have common names, they are also recorded.

Each entry includes information on the form of a plant—climber, shrub, subshrub, or herbaceous—whether it is deciduous or evergreen (winter green), and average height, pruning group, and season of flowering. Additionally, the vigour of the plant is recorded as not too vigorous, vigorous, moderately vigorous, very vigorous, strong or weak growing, or compact, as the case may be.

Flower color of many clematis can be variable and depends on flowering time, composition of soil, aspect (light or shade), and temperature. Every effort has been taken to ensure the true color of the flower was captured by the photographers at the height of flowering season (main display) of each cultivar or species.

The size of flowers is also governed by several factors including soil, climate, and regular feeding and watering. The average bloom size given is for plants grown with great love and care. Although most entries give the diameter of flowers, where necessary the average length of tepals is also recorded.

Most clematis grow well in good garden soils. When other factors are important, such as grit, compost, pH, or moisture, these are clearly indicated in the descriptions. Many clematis will grow in any aspect, or planting position, in the garden, but some are better when facing north, south, east, or west. Some prefer a sheltered position, others tolerate an exposed site.

Many of the clematis described are universally hardy. Some, however, are only half-hardy (hardy from Zones 7 up) and therefore are appropriate for gardens not subjected to excessive cold or frost. Take special care with such clematis and grow them as conservatory plants or in containers which can be moved or given adequate shelter and protection during winter months.

Of the four main awards mentioned in this book, three are given by the Royal Horticultural Society. The Award of Merit (AM) is given to meritorious plants exhibited at the Society's shows including the Chelsea Flower Show. The First Class Certificate (FCC) is more prestigious than the AM and is only given to plants which are outstanding at exhibition. The Award of Garden Merit (AGM), reinstituted in 1992, is presented to plants of outstanding excellence and is of practical value for the gardener. The fourth award, given by the British Clematis Society, is the Certificate of Merit awarded to exceptional cultivars from the Society's trial grounds.

CONTENTS

Opposite: *Clematis* 'Asao'. Photo by S. Marczyński.

PREFACE

In spite of decreasing leisure time and gardening spaces, notably in urban areas, gardening continues to flourish as a major hobby. Gardeners of all age groups have their lists of favourite plants, and clematis continues to feature among the top five. That is good news indeed; however, with an ever-increasing number and variety of clematis plants available to gardeners, it is not easy to choose the right plant for the right place. That is why this pocket guide to clematis is necessary. Furthermore, the size of this guide is such that you will be able to carry it around with you to nurseries and garden centres or even when visiting other private and public gardens to help you with selection and identification of clematis.

When we embarked on growing clematis, few comprehensive books were available to us. Through patience, trial and error, and our passion for clematis, we succeeded in growing these plants. Now, we are happy to pass on our experience and joy of growing clematis to you. We believe this book will enable gardeners, specifically those who are new to gardening with clematis, to select their plants quickly and carefully according to their preferences with regard to growth habit, size and color of flowers, and thus derive maximum joy with minimum effort.

Between us we have grown many of the clematis in this book in our gardens in Ireland and England. Some of these old, tried-and-tested, widely grown plants are our firm favourites and will continue to reign supreme and enjoy pride of place in our gardens. We have also been finding room for many newcomers from different parts of the world. A large number of these carry desirable credentials and have not failed to surprise, impress, and delight us. Thus, the newcomers have earned a place in this guide.

Our selection also includes a number of plants we have admired in other people's gardens—local, national, and international. We have learned a great deal about successful gardening with clematis from many passionate clematophiles in Denmark, Estonia, Germany, Finland, Japan, Latvia, Netherlands, New Zealand, Poland, Sweden, the United Kingdom, and the United States. We are grateful to these individuals for enthusiastically sharing their experience and expertise with us.

It has not been easy to select 300 species and cultivars or to limit the amount of botanical and horticultural information on each clematis. This pocket guide is a derivative of our larger and more detailed Timber Press publication, *An Illustrated Encyclopedia of Clematis* (2001). We proudly call this smaller edition a "mobile" guide to clematis. Please do not leave home without it.

We are deeply indebted to Linda Willms of Timber Press for her meticulous attention to detail in editing, invaluable advice, help, encouragement, and support with the original encyclopedia and with this pocket guide. Our thanks also to Timber Press for making both books available to clematis fans across the world.

We wish each of you happy gardening with clematis and believe that you will have no difficulty growing any of the clematis featured in this guide. Careful selection, cultivation, judicious pruning—never let that tax your mind—along with a modicum of patience and diligence will pay handsome dividends. Should you get smitten by this magical genus of plants and wish to expand your clematis collection, consider investing in our encyclopedia.

Just remember there is always room for yet another clematis in your collection. Go on, pick up a plant or two, and have fun.

Opposite: *Clematis* 'Kacper' (Caspar). Photo by S. Marczyński.

INTRODUCTION

The genus *Clematis* boasts more than 1000 species and cultivars. Many produce large, striking, and colorful semi-double and double flowers; others distinguish themselves with small, single, dainty, and charming displays of flowers.

Clematis in the Landscape

Clematis can be grown in many different ways to add to the design, elegance, and beauty of any garden. Typically, they are grown on supports. Many trees, shrubs, roses, and conifers make excellent living supports for clematis. Before planting clematis with such living hosts, however, consider the vigour, flowering times, and pruning requirements of both plants. Some pairings are not advisable: a very vigorous clematis with a compact, less vigorous supporting plant, and vice versa; an evergreen clematis with a shrub or a

climber that requires annual pruning; and any clematis with a hedge that needs regular clipping and maintenance. Roses are natural companions of clematis and have similar cultural requirements.

Walls, fences, and various free-standing artificial supports also enable clematis to make their vertical journey with ease and to show off their flowers. Attach plastic-coated wires or wooden trellises to walls and fences so that the modified leaf stalks of clematis can wrap themselves and grow away. When hanging a trellis on a wall, leave at least 2.5 cm (1 in.) between the wall and trellis by attaching blocks of wood to the wall and fastening the trellis to the blocks with rustproof screws. This space ensures enough room for air circulation, thus preventing the plants from being attacked by mildew. Passing showers of rain seldom reach the base of a wall, where the soil can

Clematis 'Praecox' is an excellent groundcover plant for larger spaces in the landscape. Photo by E. Leeds.

Opposite: *Clematis montana* var. *rubens* 'Tetrarose' finds support on *Pinus nigra* (black pine). Photo by C. Chesshire.

Clematis 'Marjorie' produces masses of flowers and makes a superb covering for a sunny pergola or roof. Photo by M. Toomey.

be very dry, so plant clematis at least 30–45 cm (12–18 in.) away from the base and enrich the planting hole with organic matter.

Many clematis may also be grown as groundcover plants or trained along the ground. Plant these in the usual way and route the stems horizontally. Use hairpins made from sturdy wire to hold the stems in place on the ground. Strong-growing clematis, for example, *Clematis montana* and its early-flowering cultivars, and the late-flowering hybrid *C.* 'Praecox', may also be grown as groundcover plants, provided adequate garden space is available.

The not-too-vigorous and compact species and cultivars are excellent container plants. Although many clematis come with labels that read "Suitable for containers," gardeners should beware.

Planting Clematis in the Garden

When purchasing a clematis, select a good, strong-growing, healthy plant. Look for two- or three-year-old bushy plants well established in good-sized pots, preferably about 2 litres (ap-

proximately ½ gallon), with two or three strong basal stems. The more basal stems per plant, the quicker it is to establish a handsome framework.

Potted clematis can be planted any time of year. Early to midautumn is ideal. The upper layers of soil are usually warm and moist, and enable the roots to grow quickly and establish themselves before the onset of winter. The next ideal season in which to plant clematis, especially the tender or evergreen varieties, is early to midspring. As soil and air temperatures begin to rise, new plants establish quickly.

Evergreen and tender varieties of clematis need a warm, sheltered position in the garden. Some forms can only be grown under glass. Pale-colored flowers tend to be bleached in strong sunlight and are best suited for growing in shade or part shade. Large-flowered clematis require protection from wind damage, and scented clematis perform better in sunny sites, although they demand a regular water supply.

Clematis thrive in fertile, loamy soil with balanced nutrients and adequate moisture. To improve clay soil, add coarse horticultural grit or sharp sand. To improve sandy soil, add humus (organic matter). Well-rotted farmyard or horse manure, garden compost, leaf-mould, mushroom compost, or good-quality, proprietary, soil-based potting compost are excellent materials for enriching the soil.

Although clematis are known to thrive in alkaline soils (pH value more than 7), they also grow satisfactorily in neutral to acid soil (pH value of 7 or below). To increase soil alkalinity, add lime (calcium carbonate) to the soil far in advance of planting. Do not add lime with farmyard manure, as it reacts with the manure to release ammonia, which may damage the plants.

When planting a clematis in the garden, dig a hole at least twice as wide as the pot in which the plant is growing and at least twice as deep again. A hole 45 by 45 cm (18 by 18 in.) or larger is ideal for accommodating organic matter below and around the root ball, giving the clematis a good start for healthy growth. Loosen the base and sides of the hole gently with a garden fork. If the soil is heavy clay, place some coarse grit or sharp sand mixed with the soil at the bottom of the hole before placing any organic material in it. This improves drainage and prevents waterlogging. Place some well-rotted manure, leaf mould, or compost at the base of the planting hole to a depth of at least 10 cm (4 in.). To prevent the plant roots from becoming burned or damaged through direct contact with the manure or compost, cover the manure or compost with top soil and peat or peat substitute.

Immerse the container in which the plant is growing in a bucket of water for 10 to 15 minutes to thoroughly wet the compost and allow the roots to absorb water. Ease the plant with its cane support out of the container and gently loosen the roots at the bottom of the root ball to encourage quick growth into the surrounding soil. Place the root ball in the prepared planting hole.

If the plant produces large flowers, ensure that the surface of the root ball is at least 6 cm (2.25 in.) below the rim of the hole. Deep planting encourages large-flowered cultivars to develop a

Clematis 'Madame Julia Correvon', like other cultivars of *C. viticella*, is not susceptible to clematis wilt. Photo by S. Marczyński.

healthy basal root crown of buds below the soil level as a precaution against sudden wilting. Such planting is unnecessary for *Clematis alpina*, *C. tangutica*, *C. viticella*, and their cultivars because they generally do not succumb to wilt. Similarly, evergreen and herbaceous species such as *C. armandii*, *C. cirrhosa*, *C. heracleifolia*, *C. integrifolia*, and *C. recta* should be planted with the crown of the plant level with the soil.

When the plant is in position, fill the area around the root ball with equal parts of good soil and potting compost mixed with the recommended amount of any general-purpose fertilizer.

Gently firm the mixture around the root ball. Cover the base of the plant with additional organic matter, taking care to keep it away from the stems or vines. Water the plant well, allowing at least 4 litres (about 1 gallon) of water per plant. Finally, attach a permanent label to the plant with the name of the clematis, pruning group, and date of planting.

To provide some shade for the plant's root system and to prevent excessive loss of moisture, plant a low-growing perennial or shrub close to

Clematis macropetala is ideal for large containers as it produces many spring flowers and requires little or no pruning. Photo by M. Toomey.

the newly planted clematis. Avoid using slates, slabs, or tiles to shade the clematis roots as these also provide hiding places for slugs, snails, woodlice, and other insect pests.

Pruning

The main reasons for pruning clematis are to establish a neat and tidy framework, to encourage vigorous growth, and to stimulate the development of buds and flowers. Most newly planted clematis need to be pruned back to at least 30 cm (12 in.) from the ground in the spring following the initial planting. This pruning encourages plants to produce new shoots from lower down the stems and from below the soil surface; however, certain evergreen and tender varieties, such as *Clematis armandii, C. forsteri, C. paniculata,* and their cultivars, should not be severely pruned provided the plants are strong, bushy, and healthy.

In areas with harsh winters, especially when snow cover is absent and temperatures fluctuate unpredictably, pruning is best done in midspring. Gardeners in coastal and temperate regions can begin pruning in midwinter or even late autumn.

Established clematis plants fall into three major pruning categories. Whether plants are grown in a container or in the garden, the pruning procedures are the same.

Pruning Group 1

Evergreen and deciduous clematis that flower on old ripened wood during winter or early to late spring do not require any major pruning. A simple rule for these is this: If a clematis flowers before early summer, do not prune it. All winter- and spring-flowering *Clematis* species and their cultivars need little or no pruning, including *C. alpina, C. armandii, C. cirrhosa, C. forsteri, C. macropetala, C. napaulensis,* and *C. paniculata.* If, however, the plants have outgrown their allocated space or become overgrown and untidy, a certain amount of cutting back and tidying up may be undertaken after the flowering period has ended. Ideally, pruning to maintain a plant's handsome framework should be done annually.

Pruning Group 2

Some clematis produce two flushes of flowers. The first display appears before early summer on old growths made during the previous year(s); the second display appears during late summer on new growths made in the current year. Most clematis with double or semi-double flowers belong in this group. These plants do not require major pruning, but all dead and weak stems should be removed in late spring. If a certain amount of selective pruning is necessary, it may be undertaken immediately after the early flowering period is over, starting from the top of the plant and working downwards. It is also desirable to prune back the flowered shoots to encourage a second display of flowers. The general rule for pruning clematis in group 2 is this: To avoid loss of early flowers, do not indulge in large-scale pruning of old wood made during the previous season(s).

Pruning Group 3

Clematis species and cultivars that flower on the current year's new growth after early summer are commonly referred to as midsummer- to late-summer-flowering clematis. These plants need annual pruning in late winter or early spring, or even later in the season, depending on when spring arrives. Among this group are *Clematis integrifolia*, *C. tangutica*, *C. viorna*, and *C. viticella*, as well as some of the large-flowering cultivars. These clematis must be pruned very hard.

A rapid and easy method of pruning these clematis is to start at the base of the stems and work upwards to the first pair of healthy, plump buds. Prune the stems just above these buds, and remove all old growths above the cuts. At times such buds may not be easily visible, so look for the nodal points of the leaves and cut just above those to remove all old growths. Such severe pruning encourages plants to produce strong new shoots and to flower very well. The general rule for pruning clematis in group 3 to cut back all the old stems to the lowest pair of live buds.

Partial and Optional Prunings

Certain well-established *Clematis* species and cultivars, including *C.* 'Helios' (Aztek), *C.* 'Huldine', *C.* 'Kugotia' (Golden Tiara), and *C. tangutica*, may be partially pruned to produce a continual display of flowers. To achieve this, hard prune only half of the old stems or vines (from the previous years' growths), allowing the unpruned half to come into flower early in the season. When the old growths have stopped flowering,

Clematis 'Huldine' produces outstanding white flowers on both old and new wood and can be pruned to provide a profuse display of blooms lasting up to five months. Photo by S. Marczyński.

new growths will come into flower, thus ensuring a continuous display of flowers on a single plant.

Nursery catalogues and plant labels often indicate that pruning of a particular clematis may be optional or done as for pruning groups 2 or 3. Examples of such plants are *Clematis* 'Carnaby', *C.* 'Ernest Markham', *C.* 'Huldine', and *C.* 'Lady Betty Balfour', which flower on both old and new wood. If these clematis are not pruned or are only lightly pruned, they will produce early flowers on old wood. If, however, they are pruned very hard, the flowering period will be delayed by at least six weeks, and the plants will remain somewhat compact.

Pruning Herbaceous, Semi-herbaceous, and Woody Clematis

Herbaceous clematis, such as *Clematis* ×*aromatica*, *C. heracleifolia*, and *C. integrifolia*, can be treated just like other herbaceous perennials in the garden. With the onset of very cold winter, almost all the soft top-growth of these clematis dies back to ground level. Where winters are mild, the process of dying back may not be complete. In this case, cut the top-growth down to ground level towards the end of winter or beginning of spring. Semi-herbaceous and woody subshrubs, such as *C.* ×*durandii* and *C. recta*, can be pruned just like herbaceous clematis by cutting the old semi-woody and woody top-growth to ground level towards the end of winter or beginning of spring.

Pruning Companion Clematis

Clematis grown with shrubs, trees, roses, conifers, heathers, and other climbers should not be hard pruned if they belong to pruning group 1 or 2. If they belong to pruning group 3, however, they can be pruned in two easy steps. Cut away all the top-growth of deciduous climbing clematis after the leaves have fallen, leaving about 2 m (6.5 ft.) of stems so that the natural supports can come into their own during winter. Complete the final pruning in early spring.

Pruning Unidentified Clematis

Occasionally, the identity of a clematis plant is unknown, making it difficult to determine its pruning category. The label may have been lost or perhaps the plant is an established one in a recently acquired garden. Where the name of the plant is unknown, especially in an old garden, do not rush the pruning. Seek help from an experienced clematis gardener or assign a number to each plant and observe its flowering pattern over 12 months, recording the details of the flowering period. Using the pruning guide in this chapter, assign the plants to their respective pruning groups and maintain them accordingly.

Cultivation and Care of Clematis in the Garden

Soon after pruning, mulch, feed, and water the plants. Mulch them generously with well-rotted farmyard manure or compost. Scatter the recommended dosage of a general-purpose granular fertilizer plus a handful of bone meal on the mulch and fork them in. Water in the fertilizer.

Provide regular watering throughout the growing season, particularly during dry spells. As plant growth becomes vigorous with rising air and soil temperatures, feed the plants at least once a month with a general-purpose liquid fertilizer. Foliar feed benefits the leaves, but a high-potash tomato feed, used in place of the general-purpose liquid feed during mid to late spring, encourages flowering.

When flower buds are ready to open, stop feeding so as to prevent all the buds opening in quick succession, thereby shortening the flowering period. Recommence feeding when flowering is completed to invigorate the plants and encourage another flush of flowers, particularly in repeat-flowering cultivars. Taper off feeding and watering by midautumn.

Clematis which flower on old wood before late spring or even slightly later in the season; single, large-flowered cultivars such as *Clematis* 'Asao', *C.* 'Dawn', and *C.* 'Miss Bateman'; and all double and semi-double varieties should not be fed inorganic fertilizers until their flowering period is over.

Soon after flowering, plants can be cleaned up by removing dead or weak stems and by cutting back some old wood in well-established plants which may look untidy or which need to be kept within bounds. Feed the plants with a general-purpose inorganic fertilizer.

Continue feeding them with a liquid fertilizer, but stop feeding those plants which may produce a second crop of flowers later in the season as soon as buds are plump and ready to open. Recommence feeding these plants after flowering, but halt the feeding programme during late summer or early autumn.

Certain winter-flowering evergreen clematis, such as *Clematis cirrhosa* var. *balearica* and *C. napaulensis*, may go into a state of dormancy (no active growth) for a period during summer. Such plants need not be watered regularly or fed during that time. Instead, begin the routine care of watering and feeding as plants awake from their dormancy, usually late summer. Refrain from overwatering clematis from regions accustomed to a certain amount of dry conditions, such as the Mediterranean, parts of the United States, and New Zealand.

Transplanting Established Plants

Relatively young plants can be transplanted more successfully than older, more mature plants, and are best moved in late winter when plants are dormant. Plants with thin, fibrous roots are easily damaged, so be very careful when moving them. Evergreen clematis are best transplanted in spring or from late summer to early autumn. For all clematis, the general rule is to transplant them after flowering.

Clematis 'Kardynal Wyszyński' (Cardinal Wyszynski) is among the spectacular, easy-to-grow clematis recommended for beginning gardeners by the International Clematis Society. Photo by S. Marczyński.

Before transplanting, reduce the bulk of the stems or vines by pruning them down to within at least 60 cm (24 in.) of the soil level, even if it means loss of flowers in deciduous clematis which flower on the previous season's old wood. In the case of evergreen clematis, completely remove some stems and thin the plant before transplanting.

To transplant an established clematis, first insert a long bamboo cane near the plant and tie all the vines or stems to it. Using a spade, dig a circle around the plant at least 30–45 cm (12–18 in.) from its base. Repeat this operation a few times to cut all roots and free the root ball from the surrounding soil.

Placing the spade under the root ball, gently lift it to make sure all roots have been cleanly cut. Place the root ball on a heavy-duty polyethylene sheet or burlap sack and keep covered and moist until it reaches the new site.

Follow the procedure outlined for planting new clematis, and ensure that the planting hole is wide and deep enough to receive the root ball with the shortened stems. Remember to plant it 6–7.5 cm (2.25–3 in.) deeper than the previous soil level, particularly if it is a large-flowered cultivar.

Water the plant immediately after replanting. Then untie stems from the temporary cane support, and tie them to their permanent support or to the host plant through which the clematis is to grow. Spray foliage with water at regular intervals to reduce evaporation.

Pinching-out

Pinching-out involves removing the growing tips of a plant to force the development of side shoots. Leggy or weak-growing clematis plants benefit from this action, although care should be taken to stop pinching-out about six weeks before flowering time begins. Otherwise, the process interferes with the development of flower buds. Through trial and error, the art of pinching-out can be perfected to achieve a handsome plant with a generous display of shoots, buds, and flowers.

Cultivation and Care of Clematis in Containers

Most clematis in containers cannot be expected to give a good account over many years. Regular care and maintenance are primary requisites for successful container culture of clematis, even if it is only for a short term.

Oak barrels and other wooden containers, as well as those made from stone or concrete, are ideally suited for growing clematis. Invest in good-quality, wide-mouthed, wide-based con-

Clematis 'Markham's Pink' produces best flower color in sun and may be allowed to roam into medium-sized shrubs or small trees. Photo by Mary Toomey

tainers measuring at least 45 by 45 cm (18 by 18 in.) with good depth and adequate drainage holes.

A mixture of soil-based and soil-less compost is ideal for container culture. Garden soil is not recommended as it becomes compact and interferes with drainage. Place a layer of small stones, pebbles, or coarse grit over drainage holes to prevent them from being blocked by the compost. Fill the container with a proprietary compost, scooping enough from the centre of the container to accommodate the root ball. After immersing the plant in a bucket of water for about 15 minutes, ease it out of its pot and place the root ball in the planting hole. Fill the area around the root ball with compost and gently firm it. Any remaining space should be similarly filled, but leave at least 5 cm (2 in.) of space below the container rim to facilitate easy watering. Insert a slow-release fertilizer plug into the compost, following the recommendations given for its application, and water the plant gently but thoroughly. Plant a few annuals or a compact, low-growing perennial at the base of the clematis to provide shade and to conserve moisture. Alternatively, place a layer of horticultural grit or gravel on the surface of the compost.

Container-grown clematis need support from the time of planting. Place the support securely in the container and train the stems onto it. Tying-in stems to the support and training the plant well from the bottom up will create a beautifully grown plant.

It is important to limit wind rock of container plants as it may cause stem or root damage.

As well as routine care—watering, feeding, training, and tying-in new growths from spring through early autumn—container-grown clematis need extra attention. In open gardens, with the possible exception of very mild or sheltered maritime gardens, clematis do not enjoy the wetness, very low temperatures (-10°C or 14°F), or strong, cold winds of winter, so every care should be taken to shelter these plants from the elements until the arrival of warm weather. If feasible, move the containers into a glasshouse, well-lit garage, outhouse, shed, or porch or position containers at the base of a south-facing wall for protection.

Should the containers prove too heavy to move and, if the plants are hardy, prune away the top one-third of the stems and tie-in the rest to their supports to prevent wind rock and to protect the roots. A thick mulch gives added protection to the roots. If these clematis flower on ripened old wood, there will be some loss of flowers the following year.

Non-hardy plants in containers too heavy to move should be wrapped in place to prevent excessive winter damage and loss. Wrap the plants with layers of horticultural fleece, and the containers with bubble wrap. Keep the compost slightly moist. During late winter or early spring, remove the horticultural fleece and prune the plants as necessary. Re-cover the clematis until all danger of frost has passed.

Plants that overwinter in containers should be repotted in spring or, at least, have their compost replenished. Simply remove the top 7.5–10 cm (3–4 in.) of compost, and replace it with a mixture of two parts loam-based potting compost and one part peat or suitable peat alternative. Ensure that the plant is supported securely, water it thoroughly, and commence feeding.

The best time for repotting clematis is early to late spring. If the plant needs pruning, do so before repotting. Carefully ease the root ball out of the container and move it to a larger pot filled with fresh potting compost. Firm the plant in, and water it.

If the container is very large, lay it on its side and run a long-bladed knife between compost and container to loosen the root ball and ease out. If the mouth of the container is not wide enough for the root ball to pass through, use a carving knife or similar implement to cut the outer 5–7.5 cm (2–3 in.) of the root ball before removing it. Once the root ball is out of the container, it may be necessary to reduce its size by cutting off 5–7.5 cm (2–3 in.) of roots, or even more from the outer edges. This is known as root pruning.

When repotting, refrain from forcing the plant out of its container by stems. Prune away at least one-third of stems of clematis which flower on old wood, even if it means loss of flowers during the following season. Clematis with good, strong roots seldom die. If the clematis is too big for a container, plant it in the open garden and start over with a young plant.

Pests and Diseases

The symptoms of snails and slugs include irregular holes in the leaves, chewed flower bud and tepals, stripped stems which appear almost white. Young clematis shoots are particularly prone to such damage. Remove the snails and slugs by hand.

Aphids are winged or wingless insects found in clusters on stems, buds, and the undersides of leaves. Symptoms include stunted and distorted leaves and blackened or sticky stems. Apply insecticidal soap, adhering strictly to label instructions, or regularly hose off with a stream of water.

Mildew is a fungal disease to which certain *Clematis* cultivars are more susceptible than others. It spreads rapidly in dry mild weather and in conditions of shade and poor air circulation. The fungal growth, usually white and powdery, appears on leaves and stems. Leaves become yellow and drop early, the plant looks unsightly, and in very severe cases of infection buds and flowers may become distorted. To avoid mildew, mulch and water regularly, specifically around the base of the plant. Avoid wetting leaves when watering. Encourage air circulation by having a good air space between the trellis and the wall.

Wilt is an important fungal disease of clematis. Large-flowered cultivars vary in their susceptibility to wilt, but the small-flowered species and cultivars are usually resistant to the disease. Symptoms of the disease include sudden wilting and collapse of either a previously healthy stem(s) with or without buds and flowers, or even the whole plant. Wilted stems appear black and eventually die back. To control this disease, cut back the wilted stems below the level of infection or, if necessary, at ground level. Remove infected material as the fungus can survive in dead plant material for many months and can be dispersed by water or insects. Thoroughly disinfect any tools used to cut back wilted plants. If a plant succumbs to wilt year after year, remove and discard the whole plant and replace the soil before planting a new clematis. No effective chemical treatment is currently available.

Clematis 'Blekitny Aniol' (Blue Angel) has a long flowering season and low water requirements, making it ideal for container culture. Photo by S. Marczyński.

Clematis Groups

The grouping of clematis used here is based on John Howell's article, "A Gardener's Classification of Clematis," published in *The Clematis* (1992, p. 34). The large-flowered group, consisting of cultivars only, is known for its large, open, rarely scented flowers. It is further subdivided into early and late-flowering groups. Early flowering cultivars produce flowers on old wood from the previous year and therefore require little or no pruning in early spring. Late-flowering cultivars produce their flowers on new growth from the current year and therefore should be pruned hard in spring to encourage new shoots.

The small-flowered group includes species and cultivars with numerous small, often scented flowers. Like the large-flowered group, the small-flowered clematis are divided into early and late-flowering kinds. The early flowering types are further subdivided into Evergreen, Atragene (Macropetala, Alpina, and Koreana), and Montana Groups, and the late-flowering types into Herbaceous, Viticella, Tangutica, Texensis-Viorna, and Vitalba Groups.

The Evergreen Group includes *Clematis armandii*, *C. cirrhosa*, and *C. forsteri* and their cultivars, all popular with gardeners because their foliage and flowers brighten the winter months. Many require shelter from wind and frost, and most make excellent conservatory and glasshouse plants.

The Atragene Group (*Clematis alpina*, *C. macropetala*, *C. chiisanensis*, *C. koreana*) comprises deciduous woody climbers with single bell-shaped flowers. These trouble-free, easy-to-grow clematis grow well in sun or shade. Among them are hardy plants suited for cold, exposed gardens. The main difference between *C. alpina* and *C. macropetala* is that the flowers of the former carry four tepals while those of latter are either semidouble or double.

The Montana Group (*Clematis montana*), although not fully hardy in cold climates, is an easy group to grow elsewhere for the sheer abundance of its late-spring flowers. It is particularly popular in the British Isles and Ireland.

Unlike most clematis which are climbers, members of the Herbaceous Group (*Clematis heracleifolia*, *C. integrifolia*) clamber. Because they are either herbaceous or subshrubby, their topgrowth dies back each winter. The next season they produce new shoots from rootstocks or a woody base. These clematis can be grown in a border among other perennials.

The Viticella Group (*Clematis viticella* and its cultivars) consists of vigorous, hardy, floriferous plants with semi-nodding to nodding flowers. Most are wilt-resistant. Some make excellent ground covers.

The Tangutica Group (*Clematis tangutica* and its cultivars) is noted for its waxy smooth, yellow, lantern-shaped flowers which are produced continuously from early summer through autumn. They also produce attractive, relatively large, silky seedheads.

The Texensis-Viorna Group (*Clematis texensis*, *C. viorna*, *C. crispa*) comprises semi-herbaceous to herbaceous climbers with small tulip-like or bell-like flowers. They can be grown like other herbaceous garden perennials; however, they need some support.

The Vitalba Group (*Clematis ligusticifolia*, *C. potaninii*, *C. vitalba*, *C. virginiana* and their cultivars) consists of deciduous woody climbers noted for an abundance of single, small white to pale yellow flowers produced in late spring and summer to autumn.

CLEMATIS
FOR SPECIFIC PURPOSES AND LOCATIONS

The lists that follow are representative only and do not include every clematis described in this guide. The lists of early- and late-flowered plants with large and small blooms are based on the *Clematis for Beginners List*, published by the International Clematis Society (2004). Ideas for growing clematis in a garden setting may be gleaned from the "Mary Toomey Clematis Display Garden" at Chalk Hill Clematis Farm, Healdsburg, California.

Early Small-flowered Clematis

C. alpina
C. 'Broughton Star'
C. 'Constance'
C. 'Frances Rivis'
C. macropetala
C. 'Markham's Pink'
C. 'Mayleen'
C. montana var. *grandiflora*
C. montana var. *rubens* 'Tetrarose'
C. 'White Swan'

Early Large-flowered Clematis

C. 'Fujimusume'
C. 'General Sikorski'
C. 'Guernsey Cream'
C. 'Kakio' (Pink Champagne)
C. 'Mrs George Jackman'
C. 'Niobe'
C. 'Piilu'
C. 'The President'
C. 'Westerplatte'

Late Large-flowered Clematis

C. 'Ascotiensis'
C. 'Blekitny Aniol' (Blue Angel)
C. 'Comtesse de Bouchaud'
C. 'Gipsy Queen'
C. 'Hagley Hybrid'
C. 'Huldine'
C. 'Jackmanii'
C. 'John Huxtable'
C. 'Kardynal Wyszyński' (Cardinal Wyszynski)
C. 'Polish Spirit'
C. 'Prince Charles'

C. 'Ramona'
C. 'Victoria'
C. 'Viola'
C. 'Warszawska Nike' (Midnight Showers)

Late Small-flowered Clematis

C. 'Abundance'
C. 'Alba Luxurians'
C. 'Alionushka'
C. 'Arabella'
C. 'Aureolin'
C. 'Betty Corning'
C. 'Bill MacKenzie'
C. ×*diversifolia* 'Hendersonii'
C. 'Duchess of Albany'
C. ×*durandii*
C. 'Emilia Plater'
C. 'Evisix' (Petit Faucon)
C. 'Helios' (Aztek)
C. 'Kermesina'
C. 'Kugotia' (Golden Tiara)
C. 'Lambton Park'
C. 'Madame Julia Correvon'
C. mandschurica
C. 'Minuet'
C. 'Paul Farges' (Summer Snow)
C. 'Praecox'
C. 'Princess Diana'
C. 'Rooguchi'
C. 'Royal Velours'
C. tangutica
C. terniflora
C. ×*triternata* 'Rubromarginata'
C. 'Venosa Violacea' (Violet Star Gazer)
C. viticella

Opposite: *Clematis* 'Aureolin', seedheads. Photo by S. Marczyński.

Clematis with Best Red Flowers

C. 'Allanah'
C. 'Crimson King'
C. 'Corona'
C. 'Ernest Markham'
C. 'Gravetye Beauty'
C. 'Hania'
C. 'Jackmanii Rubra'
C. 'Madame Julia Correvon'
C. 'Maureen'
C. 'Niobe'
C. 'Rouge Cardinal'
C. 'Rüütel'
C. 'Ville de Lyon'
C. 'Westerplatte'

Clematis with Best Blue Flowers

C. alpina
C. 'Arabella'
C. 'Ascotiensis'
C. 'Blekitny Aniol' (Blue Angel)
C. ×durandii
C. 'Elsa Späth' (Blue Boy in Australia)
C. 'Emilia Plater'
C. 'Evisix' (Petit Faucon)
C. 'Frances Rivis' (English form)
C. 'Fujimusume'
C. 'General Sikorski'
C. 'Ken Donson'
C. 'Kiri Te Kanawa'
C. 'Lasurstern'
C. macropetala
C. 'Mrs James Mason'
C. 'Mrs P. B. Truax'
C. 'Multi Blue'
C. 'Perle d'Azur'
C. 'Prince Charles'
C. 'Sinee Dozhd' (Blue Rain)
C. 'The President'
C. 'William Kennett'

Clematis with Pink Flowers

C. 'Alionushka'
C. 'Asao'
C. 'Barbara'

C. 'Bees Jubilee'
C. 'Comtesse de Bouchaud'
C. 'Constance'
C. 'Doctor Ruppel'
C. 'Elizabeth'
C. 'Étoile Rose'
C. 'Evifive' (Liberation)
C. 'Evijohill' (Josephine)
C. 'Hagley Hybrid'
C. 'Jan Pawel II'
C. 'Kakio' (Pink Champagne)
C. 'Markham's Pink'
C. 'Nelly Moser'
C. 'Odoriba'
C. 'Piilu'
C. 'Pink Fantasy'
C. 'Princess Diana'
C. 'Rosea'
C. 'Rosy O'Grady'
C. 'Willy'

Clematis with Purple Flowers

C. 'Akaishi"
C. 'Edomurasaki' (Blue Bird)
C. 'Étoile Violette'
C. 'Evifour' (Royal Velvet)
C. 'Fireworks'
C. 'Gipsy Queen'
C. 'Jackmanii'
C. 'Kacper'(Caspar)
C. 'Monte Cassino'
C. 'Mrs N. Thompson'
C. 'Polish Spirit'
C. 'Romantika'
C. 'Rooguchi'
C. 'Star of India'
C. 'Tartu'
C. 'Venosa Violacea' (Violet Star Gazer)
C. 'Viola'
C. 'Warszawska Nike' (Midnight Showers)

Clematis with Mauvish Flowers

C. 'Barbara Jackman'
C. 'Belle of Woking'
C. 'Betty Corning'
C. 'Entel'

C. 'Evione' (Sugar Candy)
C. 'Pamiat Serdtsa'
C. 'Royal Velours'
C. 'Royalty'
C. 'Silver Moon'
C. 'Victoria'
C. viticella
C. 'Vyvyan Pennell'

Clematis with White Flowers

C. 'Alba Luxurians'
C. 'Albina Plena'
C. 'Andromeda'
C. 'Apple Blossom'
C. armandii
C. 'Bowl of Beauty'
C. 'Evitwo' (Arctic Queen)
C. flammula
C. florida var. flore-pleno
C. florida var. sieboldiana
C. 'Gillian Blades'
C. 'Henryi'
C. 'Huldine'
C. 'Jackmanii Alba'
C. 'James Mason'
C. 'John Huxtable'
C. 'Kaiu'
C. mandschurica
C. 'Marie Boisselot'
C. 'Miss Bateman'
C. 'Mrs George Jackman'
C. 'Paul Farges' (Summer Snow)
C. 'Poulala' (Alabast)
C. recta
C. 'Snow Queen'
C. 'Sylvia Denny'
C. terniflora

Clematis with Yellow Flowers

C. 'Aureolin'
C. 'Bill MacKenzie'
C. chiisanensis 'Lemon Bells'
C. chiisanensis 'Love Child'
C. 'Helios' (Aztek)
C. 'Kugotia' (Golden Tiara)
C. rehderiana

C. tangutica
C. tibetana subsp. vernayi

Groundcover Clematis

C. 'Duchess of Albany'
C. 'Gravetye Beauty'
C. 'Hagley Hybrid'
C. 'Jackmanii Rubra'
C. 'Niobe'
C. 'Pink Fantasy'
C. 'Westerplatte'

Clematis for Arches, Pergolas, Pillars, and Roses

C. 'Abundance'
C. 'Ascotiensis'
C. 'Betty Corning'
C. 'Blekitny Aniol' (Blue Angel)
C. 'Comtesse de Bouchaud'
C. 'Elsa Späth'
C. 'Étoile Violette'
C. 'General Sikorski'
C. 'Mrs Cholmondeley'
C. 'Perle d'Azur'
C. 'Polish Spirit'
C. 'Romantika'
C. 'Star of India'
C. 'Victoria'
C. 'Ville de Lyon'
C. 'Viola'
C. 'William Kennett'

Clematis for Growing Through Small Trees and Large Shrubs

C. chiisanensis 'Love Child'
C. 'Comtesse de Bouchaud'
C. 'Dorothy Walton'
C. 'Étoile de Malicorne'
C. 'Gipsy Queen'
C. 'Huldine'
C. 'Jackmanii Alba'
C. 'Jackmanii Superba'
C. 'Madame Julia Correvon'
C. 'Marie Boisselot'
C. 'Miss Bateman'
C. 'Ramona'

Clematis for Sheltered North Walls and Fences

C. 'Andromeda'
C. 'Bees Jubilee'
C. 'Carnaby'
C. 'Caroline'
C. 'Comtesse de Bouchaud'
C. 'Dawn'
C. 'Doctor Ruppel'
C. 'Fujimusume'
C. 'Guernsey Cream'
C. 'Hagley Hybrid'
C. 'John Warren'
C. 'Nelly Moser'
C. 'Poulala' (Alabast)

Clematis for Large Containers (Short-term Cultivation)

C. 'Anna Louise'
C. 'Asao'
C. 'Evitwo' (Arctic Queen)
C. 'Fujimusume'
C. macropetala
C. 'Mrs P. B. Truax'
C. 'Pink Fantasy'
C. 'Silver Moon'

Clematis for Small Gardens

C. 'Betty Corning'
C. chiisanensis 'Lemon Bells'
C. chiisanensis 'Love Child'
C. ×durandii
C. 'Entel'
C. 'Étoile Rose'
C. 'Evisix' (Petit Faucon)
C. 'Evitwo' (Arctic Queen)
C. 'Fujimusume'
C. 'Hagley Hybrid'
C. 'Kommerei'
C. macropetala
C. 'Madame Julia Correvon'
C. 'Markham's Pink'
C. 'Miniseelik'
C. 'Miss Bateman'
C. 'Niobe'
C. 'Odoriba'
C. 'Pagoda'
C. 'Perle d'Azur'
C. 'Pink Fantasy'
C. 'Polish Spirit'
C. 'Princess Diana'
C. 'Romantika'
C. 'Sylvia Denny'
C. 'Tentel'
C. 'Ville de Lyon'

Opposite: Clematis 'Comtesse de Bouchaud'
growing with *Rosa* 'Pink Bells'. Photo by R. Surman.

CLEMATIS A–Z

Clematis 'Abundance'

Viticella Group. RHS Award of Garden Merit (2002). Hardy, vigorous, deciduous climber 3–4 m (10–13 ft.) tall. Very floriferous. Pruning group 3. Flowering from mid to late summer. Single, wine-red, semi-nodding flowers are 5–7.5 cm (2–3 in.) across with four or five blunt tepals, each with darker pink veining, a lighter pink central bar, and recurved margins and tips. Ideal for a trellis, arbour, or pergola. Best grown through a tree, conifer, or large shrub with light-colored foliage. Zones 3–9.

Clematis 'Akaishi'

Hardy, moderately vigorous, deciduous climber 2.4–3 m (7.75–10 ft.) tall. Pruning group 2. Flowering from mid to late spring and again in late summer. Single, deep purple flowers, 15–20 cm (6–8 in.) across, are composed of eight boat-shaped, pointed tepals, each with wavy margins and a prominent cerise-pink central bar. Best in garden soils enriched with humus. Partner it with other wall-trained shrubs, climbers, or moderately vigorous clematis which do not require annual pruning. Zones 4–9.

Clematis 'Alba'

Herbaceous/Integrifolia Group. Hardy, non-clinging, deciduous, herbaceous perennial 0.6 m (2 ft.) tall. Pruning group 3. Flowering from early to late summer. Single, nodding, bell-shaped, scented, white flowers, sometimes tinged with blue, are freely produced on terminal shoots and upper leaf axils. Each of the four tepals is 4–5 cm

Clematis 'Akaishi'. Photo by C. Chesshire.

Opposite: Clematis 'Abundance'. Photo by J. Lindmark.

Clematis 'Alba'. Photo by C. Chesshire.

(1.5–2 in.) long, narrow, and pointed, with up-turned tips. Ridges running from the base of the tepal to the tip. Best in garden soils enriched with humus. Produces strongest scent in a sunny position. May need some support. Ideal for the front of an herbaceous border. Zones 3–9.

Clematis 'Alba Luxurians'. Photo by E. Leeds.

Clematis 'Albiflora'. Photo by J. Lindmark.

Clematis 'Alba Luxurians'

Viticella Group. RHS Award of Garden Merit (1993). Hardy, moderately vigorous, deciduous climber 3–4 m (10–13 ft.) tall. Pruning group 3. Flowering from midsummer to early autumn. Single, slightly nodding, white flowers with tips boasting a dash of green are 7.5 cm (3 in.) across and produced in great abundance. The four to six tepals have blunt, recurved tips, and on their reverse side display a hint of pearly blue with a very pale green central bar. The green shading depends on the degree of exposure to sunlight. Some midsummer flowers are completely white. Ideal to grow through medium-sized trees and conifers, over large open shrubs, or as a specimen plant on a trellis, pergola, or obelisk. Zones 3–9.

Clematis 'Albiflora'

Atragene Group. Synonym: *C. alpina* 'Albiflora'. Hardy, moderately vigorous, deciduous climber 2.5–3 m (8–10 ft.) tall. Pruning group 1. Any pruning to keep the plant tidy should be carried out immediately after the main flowering period, which is from mid to late spring. A few flowers are produced in late summer. Single, white, nodding flowers consist of four tepals, each 5 cm (2 in.) long. Well-drained soils. Suitable for north-facing and cold aspects. Produces a better second flush of flowers in a sunny location. Ideal for small gardens. Can be grown with other early flowering clematis which do not require major pruning. Zones 3–9.

Clematis 'Albina Plena'

Atragene Group. Hardy, vigorous, deciduous climber 3–4 m (10–13 ft.) tall. Pruning group 1. Flowering from late spring to early summer. Double, sparkling white, nodding, bell-shaped flowers, 6–8 cm (2.25–3.25 in.) across, are produced freely from the previous season's old wood. The four outermost primary tepals, each about 4 cm (1.5 in.) long, enclose numerous secondary petal-

Clematis 'Albina Plena'. Photo by J. Lindmark.

Clematis 'Alice Fisk'. Photo by J. Lindmark.

like sterile stamens of similar length. Thrives in sharply drained soils. Superb for a medium-sized obelisk or trellis. Zones 4–9.

Clematis 'Alice Fisk'

Hardy, weak-growing, deciduous climber up to 1.8–2.4 m (6–7.75 ft.) tall. Pruning group 2. Flowering from late spring to early summer and again in late summer. Single, pale wisteria-blue flowers are 15–20 cm (6–8 in.) wide and composed of eight pointed, textured tepals with somewhat scalloped margins. Ideal for small gardens or container culture, trained up a small to medium-sized obelisk or trellis. Good companion for other not-too-vigorous, wall-trained shrubs which do not require heavy annual pruning. Zones 4–9.

Clematis 'Alionushka'

Herbaceous/Integrifolia Group. RHS Award of Garden Merit (2002). British Clematis Society Certificate of Merit (1998). Hardy, semi-herbaceous,

Clematis 'Alionushka'. Photo by J. Lindmark.

moderately vigorous, non-clinging, shrubby perennial 1.2–1.8 m (3.5–6 ft.) tall or taller. Pruning group 3. Flowering from early summer to early autumn. Single, delicate satiny pink, nodding, bell-shaped flowers are 5–8 cm (2–3.25 in.) across with four to six deeply textured and grooved tepals. Each tepal is up to 6.5 cm (2.5 in.) long with a deeper pink central bar. Gently scalloped margins recurve and twist with age. Best in garden soils enriched with humus. If trained on an artificial support, the stems will need tying-in. May be grown through medium-sized shrubs. Zones 3–9.

Clematis 'Allanah'
Hardy, moderately vigorous but compact, deciduous climber 1.8–2.4 m (6–7.75 ft.) tall. Pruning group 3. Flowering from early to late summer. Single, bright ruby red flowers, shaded or flushed with carmine, are gappy and 15–20 cm (6–8 in.) wide. The eight tepals, each 6.5 cm (2.5 in.) long and 3.5 cm (1.25 in.) wide, are broad and blunt-

Clematis 'Allanah'. Photo by J. Lindmark.

Clematis 'Andromeda'. Photo by M. Toomey.

Clematis 'Apple Blossom'. Photo by C. Chesshire.

tipped. Leaves are somewhat hairy underneath. Best in sun or part shade. May be grown up and over prostrate shrubs and conifers, allowed to clamber in an herbaceous border, or trained up a small obelisk or low support. Zones 4–9.

Clematis 'Andromeda'

Hardy, moderately vigorous, deciduous climber 2.4–3 m (7.75–10 ft.) tall. Pruning group 2. Semi-double flowers from late spring to early summer on the previous season's old wood and single flowers during late summer on the current season's growth. The early, white, semi-double flowers are 15–20 cm (6–8 in.) across and carry an outer basal row of eight tepals and an inner row of usually six tepals. Each tepal is broad towards the base and tapering towards the tip, with a bright pink diffused stripe along the centre. Suitable in sun or part shade. Ideal for a pergola, large obelisk, or trellis. Zones 4–9.

Clematis 'Apple Blossom'

Evergreen/Armandii Group. RHS Award of Garden Merit (2002). Half-hardy to hardy, vigorous, evergreen climber to 6 m (20 ft.) tall or taller. Pruning group 1. Flowering from early to mid-spring. Single, white, saucer-shaped, scented flowers are 5–6.5 cm (2–2.5 in.) across, tinged with pink, and borne in clusters. The four to six broad tepals do not overlap. Unopened buds appear more pinky, and new leaves are bronze-colored, turning to bright, dark green. The long boat-shaped leaves show deep ribbing along their length. Prefers well-drained soils in a sunny aspect, such as a south- or southwest-facing wall. Best trained on a house or garden wall. Old leaves turn brown and drop in summer, so choose the planting position carefully. Too vigorous for a container. Zones 7–9.

Clematis 'Arabella'

Herbaceous/Integrifolia Group. RHS Award of Garden Merit (2002). Hardy, semi-herbaceous, non-clinging, compact, shrubby perennial 1.5–1.8 m (5–6 ft.) tall. Pruning group 3. Flowering from late spring to early autumn. Single,

Clematis 'Arabella'. Photo by E. Leeds.

rounded, deep blue-mauve flowers flushed with red are 7.5–9 cm (3–3.5 in.) in diameter with four to eight pear-shaped tepals which do not overlap. As the flowers mature, their overall color lightens, and textured, pinky mauve central bands and veining become apparent. Finally, all colors fade to a light blue as the flowers age. A superb plant for gardens of any size. Best grown naturally through small to medium-sized shrubs and over prostrate golden conifers. If trained against a trellis or obelisk, the stems will need tying-in. Makes a good groundcover plant. Zones 4–9.

Clematis armandii.
Photo by E. Leeds.

Clematis armandii
'Snowdrift'. Photo
by C. Chesshire.

Clematis ×*aromatica.*
Photo by E. Leeds.

Clematis armandii

Evergreen/Armandii Group. Half-hardy to hardy, vigorous, evergreen climber or scrambler to 6 m (20 ft.) tall or taller. Native to China. Pruning group 1. Flowering from early to midspring. Single, pure white, scented flowers, 5 cm (2 in.) across, have four to six tepals and are borne in clusters of three in the leaf axils. Leaves composed of three leaflets, up to 15 cm (6 in.) long and 5 cm (2 in.) wide, are pinkish bronze when young, becoming dark glossy green and leathery with age. Thrives in well-drained soils. Best against a south- or west-facing sheltered wall in a medium-sized to large garden. Old leaves turn brown and drop in summer, so site the plant carefully. Too vigorous for a container. Not for cold gardens that experience frost. Universally popular. Zones 7–9.

Clematis armandii 'Snowdrift'

Evergreen/Armandii Group. RHS First Class Certificate (1996), RHS Award of Garden Merit (1984). Synonym: C. 'Snowdrift'. Half-hardy to hardy, vigorous, evergreen climber to 6 m (20 ft.) tall or taller. Pruning group 1. Flowering from early to midspring. Single, pure white, flat flowers are 6–7.5 cm (2.25–3 in.) across and composed of four to six overlapping tepals with pointed tips. Thrives in well-drained soils. Requires a warm, frost-free location with protection from cold winds. Grow against a sheltered, warm, south- or southwest-facing wall or fence. Some of the old leaves drop in summer, so site the plant carefully. Zones 7–9.

Clematis ×aromatica

Herbaceous Group. Hardy, semi-herbaceous, not-too-vigorous, non-clinging, somewhat upright perennial 1.2–1.8 m (3.5 ft.) tall. Pruning group 3. Flowering from late spring to early autumn. Small, single, deep mauvish blue, scented flowers, 5 cm (2 in.), across, are freely produced. The four to six narrow, ribbed tepals open flat. As the flower matures, the margins of each tepal recurve and overlap each other, forming small tunnels on the reverse. Good forms are sweetly scented. Best to buy plants in flower to ascertain scent. Prefers well-drained gritty soil. Roots resent overwatering. May be grown as a specimen plant in an herbaceous perennial border where it is fully supported by artificial structures or nearby plants. Zones 4–9.

Clematis 'Asao'

Hardy, compact, deciduous climber 1.8–2.4 m (6–7.75 ft.) tall. Very floriferous when established. Pruning group 2. Flowering from late spring to early summer and again during late summer. Large, single, sometimes semi-double, deep pink flowers are 15 cm (6 in.) across and composed of usually six to eight tepals, which are much longer than broad, tapering at both ends, and slightly reflexing at the tips. Vivid color around the edges of the tepals progressively fades to almost white towards the centre with prominent pink veining. Flowers open out flat with age. Leaves become bronze-colored as they age, although they are somewhat prone to premature yellowing. Thrives in well-drained soils. Suitable for container culture, a low garden wall or fence, or a small obelisk. Zones 4–9.

Clematis 'Ascotiensis'

RHS Award of Garden Merit (1993). Hardy, vigorous, deciduous climber 3–4 m (10–13 ft.) tall. Pruning group 3. Flowering from mid to late

Clematis 'Asao'. Photo by E. Leeds.

Clematis 'Ascotiensis'. Photo by J. Lindmark.

Clematis 'Aureolin'. Photo by C. Chesshire.

Clematis 'Bagatelle'. Photo by C. Chesshire.

summer. Single, attractive, well-formed, lavender-blue to deep blue-violet flowers are 12–13.5 cm (4.75–5.5 in.) wide. Each of the four to six wavy tepals has a broad white bar on the outside, and twists and recurves as the flowers unfurl. Grow through medium-sized trees and shrubs. Team with a not-too-vigorous climbing rose. Suitable for a pergola, large obelisk, or trellis. Zones 4–9.

Clematis 'Aureolin'

Tangutica Group. RHS Award of Garden Merit (1993). Hardy, vigorous, deciduous climber 3–4 m (10–13 ft.) tall. A floriferous cultivar. Pruning group 3. Flowering from midsummer to early autumn. Single, lemon-yellow, nodding, lantern-like flowers are composed of four broad, pointed tepals, each 4–5 cm (1.5–2 in.) long. Attractive seedheads mature before the plant finishes flowering. The seedheads are carried into winter. Well-drained garden soils. Suitable for an obelisk or large trellis. May be grown through large, open shrubs or small trees. Zones 4–9.

Clematis 'Bagatelle'

Synonym: *C.* 'Dorothy Walton'. Hardy, vigorous, deciduous climber 3–3.6 m (10–11.5 ft.) tall. Pruning group 3. Flowering from early to late summer. Single, silvery lilac, gappy flowers, 10 cm (4 in.) wide, are usually composed of six to eight long, pointed tepals. Each tepal is marbled and spotted with pink and carries a darker violet-red bar. May be grown with climbing roses or other wall-trained shrubs. Zones 4–9.

Clematis 'Barbara'

Gold medal winner at the Plantarium 2002 Arboricultural Trade Fair. Hardy, moderately vigorous, compact, deciduous climber to 3 m (10 ft.) tall. Raised in Poland. Pruning group 3. If lightly pruned, it will bloom at the beginning of summer, but after a hard prune the flowers will appear late. Free-flowering for a long period, from

Clematis 'Barbara'. Photo by S. Marczyński.

Clematis 'Barbara Dibley'. Photo by R. Surman.

Clematis 'Barbara Jackman'. Photo by C. Chesshire.

Clematis 'Beauty of Richmond'. Photo by C. Chesshire.

early to midsummer and again from late summer to autumn. Single, handsome, vivid purplish pink flowers about 15 cm (6 in.) wide carry six to seven overlapping, pointed tepals with lighter spots, fading to purplish red in autumn with a deep purplish red bar. Suitable for growing over a fence, trellis, arbour, or other garden supports as well as in a large container. Zones 4–9.

Clematis 'Barbara Dibley'

Hardy, moderately vigorous, compact, deciduous climber 1.8–2.4 m (6–7.75 ft.) tall. Pruning group 2. Flowering in late spring. Very large, single, petunia-red flowers, 15–20 cm (6–8 in.) across, consist of eight closely arranged, long, narrow, tapering tepals, each with a carmine central bar and with gently scalloped margins. Best in part shade to prevent premature fading of flower color. Suitable for container culture and for growing on a small obelisk or trellis. May be grown as a companion for wall-trained shrubs which do not require severe pruning. Zones 4–9.

Clematis 'Barbara Jackman'

Hardy, moderately vigorous, compact, deciduous climber 1.8–2.4 m (6–7.75 ft.) tall. Pruning group 2. Flowering from late spring to early summer and again in late summer. Single, bluish mauve flowers are 10–15 cm (4–6 in.) wide. The eight broadly overlapping tepals taper towards the tip, each with a crimson central bar. Although their color fades to light mauvish blue with age, they retain the color of the central bar. Best in part shade to prevent premature fading of flower color. Ideal for a patio container. Suitable for an obelisk or trellis. Zones 4–9.

Clematis 'Beauty of Richmond'

Hardy, vigorous, deciduous climber 2.5–3.6 m (8–11.5 ft.) tall. Pruning optional, group 2, or group 3. A hard pruning (group 3) results in the loss of early flowers. Flowering from early to midsummer. Large, single, pale lavender-blue flowers, 15–20 cm (6–8 in.) wide, are made of six pointed tepals, each with a deep blue bar and recurving with age. Suitable for a large obelisk, trellis, or arbour. Zones 4–9.

Clematis 'Beauty of Worcester'

Hardy, moderately vigorous, compact, deciduous climber 1.8–2.4 m (6–7.75 ft.) tall. Pruning group 2. Flowering from late spring to early summer and again from late summer to early autumn. Double and semi-double, reddish purple flowers are 12.5–15 cm (5–6 in.) across and produced on the previous season's old wood. They are composed of a basal row of six tepals with rounded edges and pointed tips. There are six or seven further concentric layers of similarly shaped tepals, each layer slightly smaller in diameter than the previous one and colored midblue with a hint of pink. The reverse of each tepal carries a white central bar. Single flowers produced on new growths later in the current season carry six tepals. Some clones are not very floriferous. Best in full or part sun. Requires protection from strong winds. May be grown in a large container if given proper support, regular care, and maintenance. Suitable for a small to medium-sized obelisk or trellis. Partner it with medium-sized shrubs, such as rhododendrons which do not require major annual pruning. Zones 4–9.

Clematis 'Bees Jubilee'

RHS Award of Garden Merit (1993). Hardy, weak-growing, compact, deciduous climber 1.8–2.4 m (6–7.75 ft.) tall. Pruning group 2. Flowering from late spring to midsummer. Single, vivid mauvish pink flowers, 15–20 cm (6–8 in.) wide, carry six to eight overlapping, rounded tepals, each with a carmine central bar. Color fades with age. Seedheads are striking. Prefers

Clematis 'Beauty of Worcester'. Photo by C. Chesshire.

Clematis 'Bees Jubilee', showing strong flower color of youth. Photo by C. Chesshire.

Clematis 'Belle Nantaise'. Photo by Y. Aihara.

part shade. Slow to become established. Feed and water well for best results. Suitable for a low trellis or medium-sized obelisk. Grow through open, not-too-vigorous shrubs which do not require annual pruning, or with other clematis from pruning group 2. Zones 4–9.

Clematis 'Belle Nantaise'

Hardy, moderately vigorous, deciduous climber 2.5–3 m (8–10 ft.) tall. Pruning group 2. Flowering from late spring to early summer. Very large, single, lavender-blue flowers, 20–25 cm (8–10 in.) wide, have six sharply pointed tepals, each with crinkly margins and a slightly lighter blue central bar. Requires a sheltered position to prevent wind damage to the large flowers. May be grown as a specimen plant if given suitable support or trained through a medium to large shrub which does not require regular annual pruning. Zones 4–9.

Clematis 'Belle of Woking'

Hardy, weak-growing, deciduous climber 1.8–2.4 m (6–7.75 ft.) tall. Pruning group 2. Flowering from early to late summer. Double, silvery mauve

flowers, 10 cm (4 in.) wide, are produced on the previous season's old wood and fade to silvery grey soon after opening. There are many layers of broad yet pointed tepals. Best in full sun or part shade. Requires protection from strong winds. Suitable for container culture or for a small to medium-sized obelisk or trellis. Zones 4–9.

Clematis 'Betty Corning'

Viticella Group. RHS Award of Garden Merit (2002). Hardy, vigorous, deciduous climber 2.5–3 m (8–10 ft.) tall. A popular, delightful cultivar. Floriferous when established. Pruning group 3. Flowering from early summer to early autumn. Single, pale lilac to mauve, bell-shaped, nodding, slightly scented flowers are 5–6 cm (2–2.25 in.) long. The four tepals recurve at the margins and tips and are pale pinky mauve inside, pale pinky blue outside. Tepals are deeply veined, thus adding to the texture. Can be grown in any aspect but produces strongest scent in a sunny position, preferably in a west-facing aspect. An excellent partner with early or late-flowering

Clematis 'Belle of Woking'. Photo by C. Chesshire.

Clematis 'Betty Corning'. Photo by J. Lindmark.

Clematis 'Bill MacKenzie'. Photo by C. Chesshire.

climbing roses. Makes a handsome display when grown over a low-growing, sturdy, wide conifer. Suitable for an obelisk, free-standing trellis, or pergola. Zones 3–9.

Clematis 'Bill MacKenzie'

Tangutica Group. RHS Award of Garden Merit (1993). Synonyms: *C. orientalis* 'Bill MacKenzie', *C. tangutica* 'Bill MacKenzie'. Hardy, vigorous, deciduous climber to 6 m (20 ft.) tall. Pruning group 3. An extremely floriferous cultivar with a long flowering period from early to late summer. Single, waxy, shiny bright yellow flowers are bell-shaped, nodding, and 6–7 cm (2.25–2.75 in.) wide. The four somewhat thick and fleshy tepals are broad at the base with pointed, recurving tips. Attractive silky seedheads. Best in well-drained soil in sun or part shade. Team it with medium-sized to large trees or conifers. Suitable for a strong, large pergola, a spacious wall, or a rustic fence. Be sure to invest in a plant grown from a cutting and not from seed. Plants grown from seed and parading as 'Bill MacKenzie' are not entitled to this cultivar name. Zones 4–9.

Clematis 'Black Prince'

Viticella Group. Hardy, moderately vigorous, deciduous climber 2.4–3 m (7.75–10 ft.) tall. Pruning group 3. Flowering from mid to late summer. Single, very dark, claret-reddish black, gappy flowers are 9 cm (3.5 in.) wide. The four broad tepals have recurved tips. Suitable for a pergola, obelisk, or free-standing trellis. Partner it with a medium-sized shrub with silver or yellow foliage. Zones 4–9.

Clematis 'Blekitny Aniol'

RHS Award of Garden Merit (2002). Trade name: Blue Angel. Hardy, vigorous, deciduous climber 3–3.6 m (10–11.5 ft.) tall. Pruning group 3. An excellent cultivar with a long flowering period from early summer to early autumn. Single, pale, rosy blue flowers are 7.5–10 cm (3–4 in.) wide with four to six tepals, each deeply grooved along the centre and boasting a very slight purple hue. Tepal margins are crinkly and recurve gently. Thrives in garden soils enriched with humus. Team it with climbing roses or large shrubs. Zones 4–9.

Clematis 'Black Prince'. Photo by R. Savill.

Clematis 'Blekitny Aniol' (Blue Angel). Photo by S. Marczyński.

Clematis 'Blue Belle'

Viticella Group. Hardy, vigorous, strong-growing, deciduous climber 3–4 m (10–13 ft.) tall. Pruning group 3. Flowering from midsummer to early autumn. Single, deep violet-blue, partially nodding, fully rounded flowers, 9 cm (3.5 in.) wide,

Clematis 'Blue Belle'. Photo by C. Chesshire.

Clematis 'Blue Ravine'. Photo by C. Chesshire.

Clematis ×bonstedtii 'Campanile'. Photo by C. Chesshire.

are borne freely on new growths and are made of six tepals. Shows up well against a light background, whether over a tree, large shrub, or climbing rose, or on its own up a trellis or any other suitable support. Zones 3–9.

Clematis 'Blue Ravine'

Hardy, moderately vigorous, deciduous climber 2–3 m (6.5–10 ft.) tall. Pruning group 2. Flowering from late spring to early summer and again in late summer. Single, soft violet flowers are 15–20 cm (6–8 in.) across and open flat with seven or eight tepals, each with wavy margins and a slightly deep violet central bar with veins radiating from it. Prefers a sheltered position in sun or part shade. Grow on a fence, trellis, or arbour. Allow to climb up a small tree or scramble over shrubs which do not require pruning. Zones 4–9.

Clematis ×bonstedtii 'Campanile'

Herbaceous/Heracleifolia Group. Synonym: *C. heracleifolia* 'Campanile'. Hardy, deciduous, non-clinging, woody subshrub 0.9–1.2 m (3–4 ft.) tall. Pruning group 3. Flowering from midsummer to early autumn. Single, pale lavender-blue, tubular flowers are 2.5–3 cm (1–1.25 in.) long, with a pale whitish bar down the centre of each of the four tepals. Tips of the tepals curl backward in a loop on mature flowers. Flowers are borne from leaf axils on the top half of stems. Well-drained garden soils. Suitable for an herbaceous or mixed border. Zones 5–9.

Clematis 'Bowl of Beauty'

Evergreen/Armandii Group. Half-hardy to hardy, vigorous, evergreen climber to 6 m (20 ft.) tall or taller. Pruning group 1. Flowering from early to

Clematis 'Bowl of Beauty'. Photo by C. Chesshire.

Clematis 'Broughton Bride'. Photo by M. Brown.

Clematis 'Broughton Star'. Photo by E. Leeds.

Clematis 'Broughton Bride'

Atragene Group. Hardy, moderately vigorous, deciduous climber 2.4–3.6 m (7.75–11.5 ft.) tall. Pruning group 1. Flowering in late spring and again from early to midsummer. Attractive, single, white, semi-nodding flowers carry four tepals, each 7.5–9 cm (3–3.5 in.) long with a pointed tip. Lilac speckles on the outside of the tepals are a welcome feature. Flowers of the second flush, although not numerous, are shorter and very full, resembling a ballet skirt. Thrives in well-drained soils. May be grown as a specimen plant on elegant supports or trained through large shrubs. Partner it with other climbers which do not require severe annual pruning. Zones 6–9.

Clematis 'Broughton Star'

Montana Group. RHS Award of Garden Merit (2002). British Clematis Society Certificate of Merit (1998). Half-hardy, moderately vigorous, deciduous climber to 6 m (20 ft) tall. Pruning group 1. Flowering from late spring to early summer. Double and semi-double, deep pink flowers up to 6 cm (2.25 in.) across are freely produced. Four large outer tepals enclose many smaller inner ones. Veins of tepals are prominent and deeper pink in color. Leaves are attractive, with a bronze tinge when young, turning dark green when mature. Best in well-drained soils. Suitable for any aspect but produces best flower color in a sunny position. One of the less-vigorous montana varieties which might suit the smaller garden. Grow through medium-sized trees and conifers. Zones 7–9.

Clematis 'Brunette'

Atragene Group. Synonym: *C. koreana* 'Brunette'. Hardy, deciduous climber 2–3 m (6.5–10 ft.) tall. Pruning group 1. Flowering from early to midspring. Small, single, plum purple flowers are nodding and bell-shaped, with four textured tepals, each 3.5–4.5 cm (1.25–1.75 in.) long, with heavy ridging running from the base to the tip. Best in well-drained garden soils enriched with humus. Suitable for a small to medium-sized pergola,

midspring. Single, pure white flowers, 5 cm (2 in.) across, are bowl-shaped when young, becoming flatter as the four to six tepals mature. Leaves are bright, dark green and glossy. Prefers well-drained garden soils. Best against a warm, south- or southwest-facing wall or fence. Old leaves turn brown and drop in summer, so choose the planting site carefully. Zones 7–9.

Clematis 'Brunette'. Photo by J. Lindmark.

Clematis 'Buckland Beauty'. Photo by E. Leeds.

obelisk, or trellis. Use for container culture, gradually potting on into larger containers at least every two or three years. Zones 3–9.

Clematis 'Buckland Beauty'

Texensis-Viorna Group. Hardy, moderately vigorous, herbaceous, deciduous climber 1.6–2.4 m (5.25–7.75 ft.) tall. Pruning group 3. Flowering from late spring to late summer. Striking, single, pink-mauve, semi-nodding, solitary, pitcher-shaped flowers, 3–3.5 cm (1.25–1.25 in.) long, are borne from the leaf axils and terminal shoots. Four fleshy, deeply ribbed, fused tepals open about three-quarters along their length nearer the recurving tips. Insides of tepals are pale greenish, sides are pale yellow and thick, and tips have mauve shading. The leaf axis occasionally terminates in a slender, tendril-like structure. Thrives in well-drained garden soils enriched with humus. Prone to mildew, so plant in an open position with plenty of air circulation. Ideal

for short-term container culture. May be grown through medium-sized shrubs or trained on an obelisk or trellis. Zones 4–9.

Clematis 'Burma Star'

Hardy, moderately vigorous, compact, deciduous climber 1.8–2.4 m (6–7.75 ft.) tall. Pruning group 2. Flowering from late spring to late summer. Single, rich, velvety purple flowers are 11.5–12.5 cm (4.5–5 in.) wide with six to eight tepals boasting reddish hues along the centre. Ideal for container culture or for growing on a small obelisk or trellis. Partner it with small to medium-sized shrubs which do not require pruning. Zones 4–9.

Clematis 'Carmencita'

Viticella Group. Hardy, vigorous, deciduous climber 3–4 m (10–13 ft.) tall. A popular and very floriferous cultivar. Pruning group 3. Flowering from mid to late summer. Single, carmine-pink to dark red, nodding flowers, 6 cm (2.25 in.) across, have four to six broad tepals, each deeply veined especially along the centre and with slightly frilly, recurved margins. Suitable for any aspect, but produces the most vibrant flower color in sun or part shade. Ideal as a specimen plant supported by an obelisk or similar free-standing structure. May be grown through medium-sized trees and conifers or over large shrubs or robust climbing roses. Best over an arbour or pergola where the nodding flowers can be viewed from below. Zones 3–9.

Clematis 'Carnaby'

Hardy, moderately vigorous, compact, deciduous climber 1.8–2.4 m (6–7.75 ft.) tall. Pruning optional, group 2, or group 3. A hard pruning (group 3) results in the loss of early flowers. Flowering from late spring to late summer. Single, raspberry-pink flowers are 15–20 cm (6–8 in.)

Clematis 'Burma Star'. Photo by M. Bracher.

Clematis 'Carmencita'. Photo by J. Lindmark.

Clematis 'Carnaby'. Photo by R. Savill.

wide with six to eight slightly reflexing tepals, each with an intensely pink central bar and crimped margins. Best in part shade to prevent premature fading of flower color. Ideal for container culture. Grow through small to medium-sized shrubs or with other moderately vigorous, wall-trained shrubs or fruit trees. Zones 4–9.

Clematis 'Caroline'
Hardy, moderately vigorous, compact, deciduous climber 1.8–2.4 m (6–7.75 ft.) tall. Pruning group 3. Flowering from early summer to early autumn. Small, single, pinkish white, well-formed, firm flowers, 10–12.5 cm (4–5 in.) wide, are composed of six to eight pointed tepals which do not overlap. Each tepal has a deeper pink bar towards the base. Best in part shade to prevent premature fading of flower color. Grow over prostrate conifers and groundcover plants such as heathers, or up and over grey- or silver-leaved small shrubs. Looks well on a small arch or an obelisk as a specimen plant. May also be grown in a raised bed and the vines allowed to tumble. Suitable for container culture. Zones 4–9.

Clematis ×*cartmanii* 'Avalanche'
Evergreen Group. RHS Award of Merit (1999). Synonym: *C.* ×*cartmanii* 'Blaaval'. Half-hardy, moderately vigorous, evergreen climber 3–4.5 m (10–14.5 ft.) tall or slightly taller. Very hand-

Clematis 'Caroline'. Photo by E. Leeds.

some in flower. Pruning group 1. If growing plants under glass, prune back after flowering, leaving two or three leaf joints. Do not be faint hearted. Flowering in midspring. Single, waxy greenish white, flat, male flowers are 4–9 cm (0.75–3.5 in.) across and borne in clusters. The four to six, sometimes seven, smooth, papery, overlapping tepals are broader than long, blunt, and with slightly wavy margins. Best in gritty, well-drained soils. Suitable for growing in a large container. May be trained against a warm, sunny wall in maritime gardens. Not for gardens in cold climates where frost is a possibility. Zones 7–9.

Clematis ×*cartmanii* 'Joe'

Evergreen Group. RHS Award of Merit (1988). Synonym: *C.* 'Joe'. Half-hardy to hardy, evergreen, non-clinging, clump-forming, bushy shrub 1 m (3 ft.) tall or, if trained up and tied to a support, to 2

Clematis ×*cartmanii* 'Avalanche'. Photo by C. Chesshire.

Clematis 'Chalcedony'. Photo by C. Chesshire.

Clematis 'Chalcedony'

Hardy, strong-growing, deciduous climber 3–4 m (10–13 ft.) tall. Pruning group 2. Remove some of the early flowered shoots to encourage new growths and more flowers second time around. Flowering from late spring to early summer and again in late summer. Double, ice-blue to very pale pink flowers are 12.5–15 cm (5–6 in.) wide with 50–60, broad, pointed tepals in many layers. Most tepals have gently scalloped margins. Welcome late-summer flowers of the second flush are also double, but smaller with fewer tepals. Best in part shade. Requires protection from strong winds. Grow on a medium-sized obelisk or trellis, or as a companion for other not-too-vigorous, wall-trained shrubs which do not require early or late annual pruning. Zones 4–9.

Clematis ×*cartmanii* 'Joe'. Photo by I. Holmåsen.

m (6.5 ft.) tall. May be grown as a low mound. Extremely floriferous. Pruning group 1. Flowering from early to midspring in the garden, even earlier under glass. Single, snowy white, male flowers are 2.5 cm (1 in.) wide and borne on short stalks. Five to eight blunt, overlapping tepals recurve with age. Unopened buds are greenish, in clusters. Attractive leaves are finely dissected and glossy. Thrives in gritty soils with sharp drainage. Best in a sheltered alpine bed, or in a container in a cold greenhouse. Not suitable for very cold gardens prone to severe frost. Zones 7–9.

Clematis 'Charissima'

Hardy, moderately vigorous, deciduous climber 2.5–4 m (8–13 ft.) tall. Pruning group 2. Flowering from late spring to early summer and again in late summer. Single, pale cerise-pink flowers, 15–20 cm (6–8 in.) wide, are composed of six to eight broad, overlapping tepals which taper towards the apex and have undulating margins. Each tepal is distinguished by a deeper colored central bar and delicate veining. Best in part shade to prevent premature fading of flower color. Requires a sheltered site. Ideal for a small garden. Suitable for a medium-sized obelisk or trellis. Team it with wall-trained shrubs or fruit trees which do not require annual pruning. Zones 4–9.

Clematis chiisanensis

Atragene Group. Hardy, moderately vigorous, deciduous climber or scrambler 2–3 m (6.5–10 ft.) tall or taller. A delightful species from South Korea suited for big or small gardens. Pruning group 1. Flowering from late spring to summer. Single, pale yellowish or greenish yellow to brownish orange-yellow flowers are pendulous, nodding, and slightly flared. The flowers are solitary or borne in groups of threes, early flowers on old wood from the previous season, later flowers on new growths from the current season. Each of the four heavily ribbed tepals is 5 cm (2 in.) long, has a spur near the base similar to the spur in columbines (*Aquilegia*), and is darker colored near the base. Best in well-drained soil, especially in a container. Suitable for sun or part shade in a sheltered position. Resents overwatering during spring and summer, and prefers to be on the dry side during winter. Grow at the back of a sunny border against a wall or fence. Zones 5–9.

Clematis chiisanensis 'Lemon Bells'

Atragene Group. Hardy, moderately vigorous, deciduous, woody climber 2–3 m (6.5–10 ft.) tall. A beautiful selection. Pruning group 1. Flowering from late spring to early summer. Single, pale yellow, pendulous flowers have a dark wine-red flush at the base when grown in sun and a reduced wine-red flush when grown in shade. Most flowers are produced on the previous season's growth, but a few are produced on new growth throughout summer. Four very thick, spongy tepals are predominantly ridged and curving outward toward their wavy tips. A ring of flattened, spoon-shaped sterile stamens,

Clematis 'Charissima'. Photo by R. Surman.

Clematis chiisanensis. Photo by J. Lindmark.

about half the length of the tepals, is located between the fertile stamens and the tepals. Seed-heads about 4 cm (1.5 in.) across are very attractive silky green when young, becoming fluffy and off-white with age. Young stems, leaf stalks, and flower stalks are a shiny dark purple. Best in well-

Clematis chiisanensis 'Lemon Bells'. Photo by S. Marczyński.

drained garden soils enriched with humus. Suitable for part shade to full sun. Refrain from overwatering during growing season, and keep on the dry side during winter. Ideal for an obelisk, trellis, or small arch in a small garden. Zones 6–8.

Clematis chiisanensis 'Love Child'

Atragene Group. Hardy, moderately vigorous, deciduous climber 2.4–3 m (7.75–10 ft.) tall. Pruning group 1. Has a long flowering period from late spring to early summer and sporadically to late summer. Single, pale lemon flowers are nodding and bell-shaped. Each of the four tepals is 5–6.5 cm (2–2.5 in.) long, curves outwards at the tip, and has a spur at the base which carries on down to the tip in the form of deep ridges. These ridges are speckled with reddish brown blotches and spots. Flower stalks and main stems are a reddish dark brown color. Best in well-drained garden soils enriched with humus. Refrain from overwatering. Grow on its own or through an open, medium-sized shrub which does not require annual pruning. Zones 5–9.

Clematis cirrhosa

Evergreen/Cirrhosa Group. Half-hardy to hardy, vigorous, evergreen climber 6–8 m (20–26 ft.) tall or taller. Native to southern Europe and the Mediterranean region including Portugal and North Africa. Pruning group 1. Any pruning to keep the plant in check should be carried out on well-established plants only, immediately after the main flowering period, by cutting them back to 1 m (3 ft.) from the ground. Flowering from midwinter to early spring in most gardens, earlier under glass or in a warm, sheltered position in the garden. Small, single, nodding flowers vary in color from white to greenish white or creamy and are 4 cm (1.5 in.) long with four tepals. The tepals are covered with reddish brown–purple blotches on their insides. Leaves are an attractive dark green and glossy. Best in well-drained soils and a warm, sunny position to ripen the flowering wood. Avoid overwatering during the plant's dormant period from early to midsummer. Suitable for a pergola, trellis, rustic fence, or wall. Zones 7–9.

Clematis chiisanensis 'Love Child'. Photo by E. Leeds.

Clematis cirrhosa. Photo by J. Lindmark.

Clematis cirrhosa var. balearica
Fern-leafed clematis

Evergreen/Cirrhosa Group. Half-hardy to hardy, very vigorous, evergreen climber 4.75–7 m (15.5–23 ft.) tall. Native to Balearic Islands, Corsica, and Sardinia. Pruning group 1. Flowering from midwinter to early spring. Small, single, creamy white to greenish white, nodding, bell-shaped flowers are lemon-scented and composed of four slightly recurving tepals, each 4

Clematis cirrhosa var. *balearica*. Photo by B. Mathew.

Clematis cirrhosa var. *purpurascens* 'Freckles'. Photo by R. Evison.

cm (1.5 in.) long with maroon, purple, or orange-brown speckles on the inside. The flowers tend to turn pink with age and form attractive fluffy balls. The good-looking, finely cut leaves turn bronzy purple in winter. Best in well-drained, somewhat gritty garden soils. Avoid watering during its short, summer dormant period. Grow on a warm, south- or southwest-facing wall or fence. Not suitable for small gardens. Zones 7–9.

Clematis cirrhosa var. *purpurascens* 'Freckles'

Evergreen/Cirrhosa Group. RHS Award of Garden Merit (1993). Synonym: *C. cirrhosa* 'Freckles'. Half-hardy, very vigorous, evergreen climber 3–4 m (10–13 ft.) tall or taller. Pruning group 1. Flowering from midautumn to early spring. Single, creamy pink, nodding flowers are held on long stalks and made of four tepals, each 4–5 cm (1.5–2 in.) long, with deep red or reddish maroon speckling on the inside. Thrives in well-drained, somewhat gritty soils in a warm, sunny position. Occasionally, plants become dormant in summer before putting on new growth prior to the flowering season. Avoid overwatering particularly during the summer dormancy. Best at the back of a border on a wall or fence. Zones 7–9.

Clematis 'Columbine'

Atragene Group. Synonym: *C. alpina* 'Columbine'. Hardy, deciduous climber or scrambler 2–3 m (6.5–10 ft.) tall. Pruning group 1. Flowering from mid to late spring. Single, pale blue, nodding flowers carry four tepals, each 5 cm (2 in.) long. Best in sharply drained soil. Suitable for any aspect, especially north- and east-facing ones.

Clematis 'Columbine'. Photo by R. Surman.

Good for container culture and small gardens. Zones 3–9.

Clematis 'Columella'

Atragene Group. Hardy, moderately vigorous, deciduous climber 2–3 m (6.5–10 ft.) tall. A superb early flowering cultivar. Pruning group 1. Flowering during late spring. Single, rosy pink, nodding, bell-shaped flowers, 5–6.5 cm (2–2.5 in.) long, are borne freely on old wood from the previous season's growth. The four to five long, narrow, pointed tepals have pale, creamy white margins and prominent darker pink continuous veins running from the base to the tip. An inner skirt of pale whitish lemon stamens encircling cream filaments and yellow anthers enlivens the flowers. Best in sharply drained soil in a sunny position. Useful for container culture, at the back of a border, or for growing through medium-sized shrubs. Zones 5–9.

Clematis 'Comtesse de Bouchaud'

RHS Award of Merit (1936), RHS Award of Garden Merit (1993). Hardy, moderately vigorous, compact, deciduous climber 1.8–3 m (6–10 ft.) tall. An old, popular, floriferous cultivar. Pruning group 3. Flowering from early to late summer. Single, mauvish to shell pink flowers, 10–15 cm (4–6 in.) wide, are usually formed of six wide, well-rounded, slightly overlapping and recurving, textured tepals, each deeply veined and distinctively grooved down the centre. Ideal for growing over prostrate conifers and other groundcover or low-growing plants. Team it with suitably colored climbing roses. May be grown short term in a container. Zones 4–9.

Clematis 'Constance'

Atragene Group. RHS Award of Garden Merit (2002). Synonym: *C. alpina* 'Constance'. Hardy, moderately vigorous, deciduous climber 2.5–3 m

Clematis 'Columella'. Photo by J. Lindmark.

Clematis 'Comtesse de Bouchaud'. Photo by M. Toomey.

Clematis 'Comtesse de Bouchaud', flower detail. Photo by C. Chesshire.

Clematis 'Constance'. Photo by R. Evison.

(8–10 ft.) tall or taller. Pruning group 1. Flowering from mid to late spring. Semi-double, deep red-pink, semi-nodding flowers are 5 cm (2 in.) long. The outer layer of petal-like sterile stamens is as colorful and as long as the tepals. Best in well-drained soil. Ideal for small gardens. May be grown short term in a container. Zones 3–9.

Clematis 'Corona'

Hardy, moderately vigorous, low-growing, compact, deciduous climber 1.2–3 m (3.5–10 ft.) tall. Pruning group 2. Flowering from late spring to early summer and again in late summer. Single, rich, velvety crimson flowers, 10–15 cm (4–6 in.) wide, are borne abundantly in spring and are composed of six to eight tepals with rather blunt tips. Late summer flowers are smaller and paler in color. Best in part shade to prevent premature fading of flower color. Ideal for container culture. Suitable for a small obelisk or for growing through low shrubs and prostrate conifers. Zones 4–9.

Clematis 'Countess of Lovelace'

Hardy, moderately vigorous, deciduous climber 1.8–2.5 m (6–7.75 ft.) tall or taller. Pruning group 2. Flowering from late spring to early summer and again in early autumn. Double flowers of first flush, produced on wood of the previous season, are 15–18 cm (6–7 in.) wide and composed of an outermost layer of pale mauve tepals followed by successive smaller layers of narrower, more pointed, blue-mauve tepals. Each of the numerous tepals carries a white bar on the reverse. Single flowers are the rule later, on the current season's new shoots. Best in full sun or part shade. Requires generous feeding and mulching during early spring to flower well. May be grown in containers or on a small obelisk or trellis. Zones 4–9.

Clematis 'Crimson King'

RHS Award of Merit (1916). Synonym: *C.* 'Crimson Star' (in the United States). Hardy, moderately vigorous, deciduous climber 2.5–3 m (8–10

Clematis 'Corona'. Photo by J. Lindmark.

ft.) tall. Pruning group 2. Flowering from early to late summer. Single, occasionally semi-double, crimson red, gappy flowers are 15–20 cm (6–8 in.) wide with five to seven broad, overlapping, pointed tepals which tend to recurve along the margins as they age. Best in part shade to prevent premature fading of flower color. Protect from strong winds. Partner it with large, open shrubs which do not require annual pruning. May also be grown as a specimen plant with the aid of suitable support. Zones 4–9.

Clematis crispa
Blue jasmine, marsh clematis

Texensis-Viorna Group. Hardy, slender, semi-woody, deciduous, usually herbaceous climber to 2 m (6.5 ft.) tall. An invaluable species native to southeastern United States. Pruning group 3. Flowering from midsummer to midautumn. Single, light blue to blue purple, nodding and semi-nodding, solitary, urn-shaped, slightly scented flowers on long stalks are 3–4 cm (1.25–1.5 in.) long. The four tepals are joined at the base, have crisped or undulate margins, and recurve at the

Clematis 'Countess of Lovelace'. Photo by J. Lindmark.

Clematis 'Crimson King'. Photo by J. Lindmark.

Clematis crispa. Photo by J. Pringle.

tips, forming a complete loop. Seedheads are prominent. Prefers neutral soil conditions in the garden. Ideal for container culture or for growing through small to medium-sized shrubs. Plants grown from seed are best, although they will vary somewhat in color and perhaps size. Zones 5–9.

Clematis 'Daniel Deronda'

RHS Award of Garden Merit (1993). Hardy, strong-growing, deciduous climber 2.4–3 m (7.75–10 ft.) tall. Pruning group 2. Flowering from late spring to early summer and again in late summer. Large, dark blue-purple, star-shaped, flattish flowers are 18–20 cm (7–8 in.) wide, with eight pointed tepals, each with faint off-white lines along the centre and recurving margins. First flush of flowers may be semi-double or single; second flush is usually single. Attractive and novel spherical seedheads have a gentle twist of the seedtails at the top. Best in sun or part shade. Requires protection from strong winds. Suitable for a medium-sized obelisk, trellis, or arch. Zones 4–9.

Clematis 'Dawn'

Hardy, moderately vigorous, compact, deciduous climber 2.5–3 m (8–10 ft.) tall. Floriferous when established. Pruning group 2. Flowering from late spring to early summer, occasionally repeating in late summer. Single, pearly pink flowers, 15–20 cm (6–8 in.) wide, are composed of usually eight, sometimes six or seven, broad, overlapping tepals, each tapering to a blunt tip. Color deepens towards the margins. Leaves are bronzy when young, becoming green as they age. Best grown out of strong sunlight to prevent premature fading of flower color. Partner it with other wall-trained shrubs or climbers which do not require annual pruning. Suitable for a sheltered pergola, trellis, or arch. Zones 4–9.

Clematis ×*diversifolia* 'Blue Boy'

Herbaceous/Integrifolia Group. Synonym: *C.* 'Blue Boy'. Hardy, moderately vigorous, deciduous, non-clinging, herbaceous perennial 1.5–1.8 m (5–6 ft.) tall. Pruning group 3. Flowering from early to late summer. Single, hyacinth-blue to midblue, bell-shaped, nodding flowers are 5–7.5 cm (2–3 in.) wide, with four tepals, each with a slight silvery sheen, a delicately textured surface, and gently notched edges. Thick and dense leaves are produced from numerous shoots

Clematis 'Daniel Deronda'. Photo by E. Leeds.

Clematis 'Dawn'. Photo by C. Chesshire.

Clematis ×*diversifolia* 'Blue Boy' growing through *Rosa rugosa*. Photo by C. Chesshire.

Clematis ×*diversifolia* 'Eriostemon'. Photo by J. Lindmark.

Clematis ×*diversifolia* 'Heather Herschell'. Photo by E. Leeds.

emerging from the base. Plant in open ground and allow to scramble. Train up an obelisk or trellis, taking care to tie-in the strong-growing shoots. Not recommended as a companion for handsome trees, shrubs, or conifers because mature plants throw numerous basal shoots with thick, dense foliage. These shoots may damage the supportive plants and their leaves, in particular. Zones 4–9.

Clematis ×*diversifolia* 'Eriostemon'

Herbaceous/Integrifolia Group. Synonym: *C.* 'Eriostemon'. Hardy, deciduous, sprawling, semi-woody shrub with erect stems 1.8–2.4 m (6–7.75 ft.) tall. Pruning group 3. Flowering from mid to late summer. Single, dark purple-blue, semi-nodding, bell-shaped flowers, 6.5–9 cm (2.5–3.5 in.) across, are borne in great abundance on current year's growth. The four tepals open wide and recurve with age. Grow through other mixed border plants, prostrate shrubs, and conifers. If trained on an artificial support, the stems will need tying-in. Zones 4–9.

Clematis ×*diversifolia* 'Heather Herschell'

Herbaceous/Integrifolia Group. Hardy, moderately vigorous, deciduous, non-clinging, herbaceous perennial 1.8–2.4 m (6–7.75 ft.) tall. Pruning group 3. Flowering from early to late summer. A profusion of single, bright, warm pink, bell-shaped, nodding flowers, 7.5 cm (3 in.) across, with four twisted tepals, each deeply grooved along the centre and gently notched at the margins. Tips of the tepals recurve with age. Plant in mixed borders and allow to grow through herbaceous plants, low shrubs, or other clematis in pruning group 3. If trained on an artificial support, the stems will need tying-in. Zones 4–9.

Clematis 'Doctor Ruppel'

RHS Award of Garden Merit (1993). Hardy, moderately vigorous, compact, deciduous climber 2.5–3 m (8–10 ft.) tall. Pruning group 2. Flowers from late spring to early summer and again in late summer. Large, single, rosy pink flowers,

Clematis 'Doctor Ruppel'.
Photo by E. Leeds.

Clematis 'Duchess of Albany'.
Photo by C. Chesshire.

15–20 cm (6–8 in.) wide, are produced in abundance and are composed of six to eight overlapping tepals, each with a striking carmine central bar, gently notched to slightly wavy margins, and tapering to a point. Withstands strong sunlight. Grow through a medium-sized shrub or in a large container. Train it up a trellis or an arch. Zones 4–9.

Clematis 'Duchess of Albany'

Texensis-Viorna Group. RHS Award of Merit (1897), RHS Award of Garden Merit (1993). Hardy, vigorous, deciduous climber with semi-herbaceous stems 2.5–3 m (8–10 ft.) tall or taller. Pruning group 3. Flowering from mid to late summer. Single, clear pink, tulip-like flowers are 5–6 cm (2–2.25-in.) long and made of four to six tepals, each with a recurving tip and a darker pink central bar. Best in sun or part shade. Prone to mildew. Team with other robust shrubs or train on a sturdy support such as an arch, pergola, or trellis. Zones 4–9.

Clematis 'Duchess of Edinburgh'

Hardy, moderately vigorous, deciduous climber 1.8–2.4 m (6–7.75 ft.) tall. Pruning group 2. Flowering from early to late summer. Sumptuous, double, white flowers 10–12.5 cm (4–5 in.) wide, with tepals in several layers and tending to recurve at the tips. Early flowers may be tinged with green and are borne on the previous season's old wood; later flowers are borne on the current season's new growth. Best in sun or part shade. Protect from cold winds. Grow through other moderately vigorous, wall-trained or free-standing shrubs which do not require annual pruning. Train on a small to medium-sized obelisk or trellis. Zones 4–9.

Clematis ×durandii

Herbaceous/Integrifolia Group. RHS Award of Garden Merit (1993). Hardy, superb, strong-growing, semi-climbing, shrubby plant with herbaceous stems 0.9–1.8 m (3–6 ft.) tall. Pruning group 3. Remove some old stems when the plant is well established and forms a large clump.

Clematis 'Duchess of Edinburgh'.
Photo by C. Chesshire.

Clematis ×*durandii*. Photo by J. Lindmark.

Clematis 'Edomurasaki' (Blue Bird). Photo by J. Lindmark.

Profuse flowering over a long period from early summer to early autumn. Single, indigo-blue, semi-nodding flowers are 9–11 cm (3.5–4.5 in.) wide and have a reddish sheen. The four to six firm tepals are blunt but pointed, each prominently ribbed along the centre and recurving along the edges with age. Reverse of each tepal boasts a deep midblue bar. A striking central tuft of stamens, of white filaments shaded with blue at the base, carries golden yellow anthers. Allow to scramble naturally through mixed borders or prostrate conifers or shrubs. If trained on a trellis or other artificial support, the stems will need tying-in. Zones 4–9.

Clematis 'Early Sensation'

Evergreen Group. Half-hardy, compact, evergreen shrub to 2 m (6.5 ft.) tall. Pruning group 1. Flowering from early to midspring. Single, pure white, bowl-shaped flowers are borne on old

Clematis 'Early Sensation'. Photo by C. Chesshire.

growths in large numbers and consist of seven, sometimes six or eight, rounded yet pointed, overlapping tepals and an attractive centre of greenish cream filaments and reduced sterile anthers. Handsome, dark green leaves are deeply dissected. Requires a free-draining compost if grown in a container. Avoid overwatering. Best grown under glass in a cool greenhouse or conservatory. Zones 7–9.

Clematis 'Edomurasaki'

Trade name: Blue Bird. Hardy, moderately vigorous, deciduous climber 2.4–3 m (7.75–10 ft.) tall. Pruning group 2. Flowering from late spring to early summer and again in late summer. Single, velvety, deep purplish blue flowers, 15–18 cm (6–7 in.) wide, have six to eight broad yet pointed, overlapping tepals. Best in sun or part shade. Slow to establish itself when young. Suitable for a medium-sized obelisk or trellis. Zones 4–9.

Clematis 'Ekstra'

An Estonian cultivar well suited for gardens in cold climates. Hardy, compact, deciduous climber 1–2 m (3–6.5 ft.) tall. Pruning group 3. Flowering from mid to late summer. A profusion of fairly large, single, light blue-violet flowers, 10–14 cm (4–5.5 in.) wide, with six to seven tepals. Each tepal has a centre which gradually fades to light blue and contrasts with deep blue veins. Best in garden soils enriched with humus. Protect from strong winds. Ideal for large containers. Train on a small to medium-sized obelisk or trellis. Team it with small to medium-sized shrubs with grey or golden foliage. Zones 4–9.

Clematis 'Elizabeth'

Montana Group. RHS Award of Garden Merit (1993). Half-hardy, vigorous, deciduous climber 7–10 m (23–33 ft.) tall. Pruning group 1. An abundance of flowers from late spring to early

Clematis 'Ekstra'. Photo by E. Leeds.

Clematis 'Elizabeth'. Photo by M. Bracher.

Clematis 'Elsa Späth'. Photo by C. Chesshire.

summer, with occasional flowers in late summer. Single, satiny, pale pink, gappy flowers are vanilla-scented and 6 cm (2.25 in.) wide. There are four tepals. Leaves are bronze when young, turning to midgreen with age. Flowers have best color and strongest scent when grown in sun. Plants grown in part shade produce paler flowers bordering on white. Grow through medium-sized to large trees and conifers. Zones 7–9.

Clematis 'Elsa Späth'

RHS Award of Garden Merit (1993). Trade name: Blue Boy (in Australia). Synonym: *C.* 'Xerxes'. Hardy, moderately vigorous, compact, deciduous climber 1.8–2.1 m (6–6.75 ft.) tall. Pruning group 2. Flowering from early to midsummer and again in early autumn. Single, occasionally semi-double, rich dark blue, rounded flowers are 15–17 cm (6–7 in.) wide, smaller when borne later in the season. There are six to eight broad, overlapping tepals. Flower color fades with time to a paler mauvish blue with a hint of pink. Ideal for containers. Partner it with small low-growing shrubs which do not require annual pruning. Zones 4–9.

Clematis 'Elvan'

Viticella Group. Hardy, vigorous, deciduous climber 3–4 m (10–13 ft.) tall. A very floriferous cultivar. Pruning group 3. Flowering from mid to late summer. Small, single, purple, nodding flowers, 5 cm (2 in.) wide, are formed of four tepals, each with a diffused, pale white central bar. Tips of the tepals sometimes recurve gently. Makes an ideal specimen plant on an obelisk or trellis. Shows up well against a light background. Team it with a white- or yellow-flowered climbing rose. Zones 3–9.

Clematis 'Emilia Plater'

British Clematis Society Certificate of Merit (2002). Hardy, very vigorous, deciduous climber 2.5–3 m (8–10 ft.) tall. Pruning group 3. Profuse flowering over a long period from mid to late summer. Small, single, violet-blue flowers, 10 cm

Clematis 'Elvan'. Photo by E. Leeds.

Clematis 'Emilia Plater'. Photo by C. Chesshire.

Clematis 'Empress of India'. Photo by J. Lindmark.

Clematis 'Ernest Markham'. Photo by E. Leeds.

(4 in.) wide, are freely produced. Four broad, rather rounded tepals are semi-nodding at first but open and slightly recurve with age. Each tepal has a central bar with darker violet veins, a textured upper surface, and crimped margins. Partner it with medium-sized shrubs and climbing roses. Makes a great display on a pergola, medium-sized obelisk, or trellis. Zones 4–9.

Clematis 'Empress of India'

Hardy, moderately vigorous, deciduous climber 2.5–3 m (8–10 ft.) tall. Pruning group 2. Flowering from early to late spring and again from mid to late summer. Single flowers, 15–18 cm (6–7 in.) wide, mauvish red on previous year's old wood in spring, a deeper reddish purple on current year's new growth. Each of the six tepals has a deeper reddish purple central bar. Requires a sheltered position to prevent wind damage to the flowers. Partner it with climbing roses and other wall-trained shrubs which do not require annual pruning. Train on an arch, trellis, or obelisk. Zones 4–9.

Clematis 'Entel'

A delightful Estonian cultivar ideal for gardens in cold climates. Hardy, weak-growing, deciduous climber 2–2.5 m (6.5–8 ft.) tall. Pruning group 3. Flowering from mid to late summer. A profusion

Clematis 'Étoile de Malicorne'. Photo by J. Lindmark.

Clematis 'Entel'. Photo by E. Leeds.

of small, single, pale pinkish mauve, well-formed flowers, 8–10 cm (3.25–4 in.) wide, with six to eight tepals, each with gently notched margins and a sharp flexible tip. Best in part shade to prevent premature fading of flower color. Grow up and over medium-sized prostrate conifers or shrubs. Train on an obelisk or medium-high trellis. Attractive when allowed to tumble over a low wall or fence. Zones 4–9.

Clematis 'Ernest Markham'

RHS Award of Garden Merit (1993). Hardy, vigorous, deciduous climber 3–3.6 m (10–11.5 ft.) tall or taller. Pruning optional, group 2, or group 3. Plants that are not pruned or lightly pruned produce early flowers from old wood. Flowering in early summer and again from late summer to early autumn. Flowering period can be extended by using a combination of both pruning groups. Single, rich petunia-red, rounded flowers, 10–15 cm (4–6 in.) across, are composed of six broad, overlapping tepals which taper to a point and have crimped margins. Suitable for any aspect but produces best flowers in sun. Grow up and over medium-sized trees or large shrubs. Train on a trellis, arch, pergola, or pillar. Somewhat shy to flower in abundance in some gardens. Zones 4–9.

Clematis 'Étoile de Malicorne'

Hardy, moderately vigorous, deciduous climber 2.5–3 m (8–10 ft.) tall. Pruning group 2. Flowering from late spring to early summer and again in early autumn. Single, rich purple-blue flowers are 15–17 cm (6–7 in.) wide and made of eight broad, slightly overlapping, pointed tepals which remain cupped for some time after opening. Each tepal carries a narrow, reddish purple central bar, and the base color tends to fade as the flower ages. Reverse of each tepal is midblue with a whitish bar. Grow where the young, cupped flowers can be enjoyed. Shows up well against a light background, such as a grey- or silver-leaved shrub which does not require pruning. Zones 4–9.

Clematis 'Étoile Rose'

Texensis-Viorna Group. Synonym: *C. texensis* 'Étoile Rose'. A superb, strong-growing, floriferous plant. Hardy, vigorous, deciduous climber 3–4 m (10–13 ft.) tall. Normally herbaceous in habit with new shoots emerging from below ground level. Pruning group 3. Flowering from midsummer to early autumn. Single, light pink, nodding and semi-nodding flowers open bell shape and are 5–7.5 cm (2–3 in.) across. The four tepals

Clematis 'Étoile Rose'. Photo by J. Lindmark.

Clematis 'Étoile Violette'. Photo by J. Lindmark.

recurve at the tip. The inside of each tepal has a deep cherry pink central bar, but on the outer side the same bar has a more pronounced light pink margin. Best in sun or part shade. Produces best flower color in a sunny position. Prone to mildew. Protect new shoots at soil level from slugs and snails. Train and tie-in the shoots from the beginning if the plant is not given another shrub, small tree, or climbing rose for support. Zones 4–9.

Clematis 'Étoile Violette'

Viticella Group. RHS Award of Garden Merit (1993). Hardy, deciduous climber 3–4 m (10–13 ft.) tall or taller. Very vigorous when established. Pruning group 3. Flowering from mid to late summer. Single, velvety, dark purple, semi-nodding, somewhat gappy flowers are 6–9 cm (2.25–3.5 in.) across and are produced in great profusion over a long flowering period on current year's new growth. The four to six tepals have a sheen, especially in young flowers. Shows up well against a light background. Use as a specimen plant on an obelisk, sturdy pillar, pergola, or trellis. Grow through medium-sized trees or large shrubs. Makes a splendid companion for robust climbing roses with white, yellow, or salmon-colored flowers. Zones 3–9.

Clematis 'Evifive'

Trade name: Liberation. Hardy, strong-growing, deciduous climber 2.4–3 m (7.75–10 ft.) tall. Pruning group 2. Flowering from late spring to early summer and again in late summer. Striking, single, cerise-pink flowers are 10–20 cm (4–8 in.) wide, with eight broad, blunt-tipped, slightly overlapping tepals, each with gently notched or scalloped edges and carrying a deep cerise central band. Earliest flowers of late spring are much larger than the late summer flowers. Protect from strong winds. Partner it with small trees or medium-sized to large shrubs which do not require annual pruning. Train up a trellis or arch. Zones 4–9.

Clematis 'Evifive' (Liberation). Photo by J. Lindmark.

Clematis 'Evifour' (Royal Velvet). Photo by J. Lindmark.

Clematis 'Evifour'

Trade name: Royal Velvet. Hardy, moderately vigorous, compact, deciduous climber to 2 m (6.5 ft.) tall. Pruning group 2. Flowering from late spring to early summer and again in early autumn. A profusion of single, rich, velvety purple flowers, 10–15 cm (4–6 in.) wide, consisting of six to eight overlapping tepals, each with a reddish purple central bar. Ideal for a small obelisk or trellis in a small garden. May be grown in a large container. Zones 4–9.

Clematis 'Evijohill'

RHS Award of Garden Merit (2002). Trade name: Josephine. Hardy, compact, deciduous climber 1.8–2.4 m (6–7.75 ft.) tall. Pruning group 2. Flowering from early summer to early autumn. Sumptuous, double, lilac-pink flowers, 10–12.5 cm (4–5 in.) wide, are composed of a basal row of six to eight broad but pointed tepals, each with a tinge of green and with a deeper pink central bar. Each successive layer of tepals is slightly shorter than the previous ones, and the tepals themselves are narrower. There are no stamens. Best in full sun. Requires protection from strong winds. If green-tinged flowers are desired, plant in part shade. Spent flowers tend to look unsightly and can be removed. Train on a small obelisk or trellis. Ideal for container culture. Zones 4–9.

Clematis 'Evione'

Trade name: Sugar Candy. Hardy, moderately vigorous, deciduous climber 2.4–3 m (7.75–10 ft.) tall. Pruning group 2. Flowering from late spring to early summer and again in early au-

Clematis 'Evione' (Sugar Candy). Photo by C. Chesshire.

Clematis 'Evijohill' (Josephine). Photo by R. Evison.

Clematis 'Evipo001' (Wisley). Photo by R. Evison.

Clematis 'Evipo002' (Rosemoor). Photo by R. Evison.

Clematis 'Evisix' (Petit Faucon). Photo by E. Leeds.

Clematis 'Evitwo' (Arctic Queen). Photo by C. Chesshire.

Clematis 'Fair Rosamond'. Photo by M. Toomey.

tumn. Single, pale pinkish mauve flowers 15–18 cm (6–7 in.) across are made of six to eight pointed tepals, each with a purplish red central bar and deeper pink veins. Best in part shade to prevent premature fading of flower color. Suitable for a medium-sized pergola, arbour, or trellis. Grow through a large shrub which requires little or no pruning. Zones 4–9.

Clematis 'Evipo001'

Trade name: Wisley. Hardy, very vigorous, deciduous climber 2.5–3 m (8–10 ft.) tall. Pruning group 3. Flowering from mid to late summer. Single, violet-bluish, semi-nodding flowers, 10–13 cm (4–5 in.) wide, are borne freely over a long period. Tepals usually number four, sometimes five or six, and have crinkled margins. Admirably suited for teaming with a climbing rose. May be grown as a specimen plant on a trellis or arch. Zones 4–9.

Clematis 'Evipo002'

Trade name: Rosemoor. An extremely floriferous plant. Hardy, very vigorous, deciduous climber 2.5–3 m (8–10 ft.) tall. Pruning group 2 or 3. Flowering from late spring to early autumn. Very large, single, reddish purple flowers with delightfully contrasting yellow stamens are 12–15 cm (5–6 in.) wide and are freely produced from previous season's wood (if left unpruned or lightly pruned) and on current season's new growths. The five or six broad tepals overlap at the base and are somewhat blunt. Ideal companion for climbing roses and medium-sized shrubs with grey foliage. May also be trained on a trellis, fence, or obelisk. Zones 4–9.

Clematis 'Evisix'

Herbaceous/Integrifolia Group. RHS Award of Garden Merit (2002), British Clematis Society Certificate of Merit (1998). Trade names: Petit Faucon, New Eriostemon. Hardy, non-clinging, herbaceous perennial 0.75–1 m (2.5–3 ft.) tall. Pruning group 3. Flowering from midsummer to early autumn. Single, deep blue-violet, broadly bell-shaped flowers are nodding or semi-nodding and 7–9 cm (2.75–3.5 in.) wide. As the flower bud opens, the four to six tepals twist slightly to expose a central boss of vivid orange-yellow stamens. When the flower opens fully, the tepals become intensely blue, almost steel blue, and the stamens become creamy white. Persistent seedheads are almost silvery white. Leaves are bronze-green when young, turning dark green with age. If trained on an artificial support, the stems will need tying-in. Grow through low or prostrate shrubs and conifers. Plant in a border among other herbaceous plants which will support the stems. Zones 3–9.

Clematis 'Evitwo'

RHS Award of Garden Merit (2002). Trade name: Arctic Queen. A very floriferous cultivar that produces flowers on both old wood from the previous season and new growth from the current season. Hardy, moderately vigorous, deciduous climber 1.8–2.5 m (6–7.75 ft.) tall. Pruning group 2. Flowering from early summer to early autumn. Double and semi-double, creamy white flowers, 10–18 cm (4–7 in.) wide, turn white with age and carry a dozen or more pointed, overlapping tepals. Best in well-drained soils in sun or part shade. Requires protection from strong winds. Water and feed regularly for best results. Team it with free-standing or wall-trained plants which do not require severe pruning. Ideal for container culture. Zones 4–9.

Clematis 'Fair Rosamond'

Synonym: *C.* 'Fair Rosamund'. Hardy, moderately vigorous but compact, deciduous climber 2.5–3 m (8–10 ft.) tall. Pruning group 2. Flowering from late spring to midsummer. Single, blush white flowers are 10–15 cm (4–6 in.) wide with six to eight overlapping, pointed tepals, each with a diffused pink central bar becoming pale and almost indistinct with age. A conspicuous central boss of dark purple-red anthers contrasts well with the tepal color. Flower buds are very plump, slightly hairy, and globose. Early spring flowers may show traces of green coloring. Well-formed, rounded, golden seedheads are long lasting. Some clones may emit a scent of violets. Invest in a plant when it is in flower. Best in part shade to prevent premature fading of flower color, but requires some sun to

Clematis 'Fireworks'.
Photo by R. Evison.

Clematis flammula. Photo by C. Chesshire.

enhance the flower scent and ripen its wood to flower well. Makes a companion for plants with dark foliage which do not require annual pruning. Ideal for container culture. Zones 4–9.

Clematis 'Fireworks'

RHS Award of Garden Merit (1993). Hardy, vigorous, deciduous climber 2.5–3 m (8–10 ft.) tall. Pruning group 2. Flowering from late spring to early summer and again in early autumn. Large, single, bluish mauve-purple flowers are 18–20 cm (7–8 in.) wide with six to eight conspicuously twisted tepals, each with gently notched margins, a tip which tends to slightly recurve with age, and a bright cerise central bar. Reverse of each tepal boasts a greenish bar and mauve margins. Best in a sheltered position to prevent wind damage to the large flowers. Grow as a specimen plant on an obelisk or with other plants on an arbour, trellis, or pergola. Zones 4–9.

Clematis flammula

Synonym: *C. recta* subsp. *flammula*. A late-flowering, floriferous species. Hardy, vigorous, deciduous climber 3–4.5 m (10–14.5 ft.) tall or taller. Native to southern Europe, North Africa, and northern Iran. Pruning group 3. Flowering from late summer to midautumn. Single, pure white, strongly scented flowers, 2–3 cm (0.75–1.25 in.) across, are borne laterally and terminally in large clusters. The four, narrow, blunt-tipped tepals are covered with very fine hairs beneath. Thrives in well-drained soil. Produces the strongest scent in a sunny position. Moderately drought-resistant. Plant against a wall or fence where the scent can be enjoyed. Suitable for a pergola, arbour, or arch. Zones 4–9.

Clematis florida var. *flore-pleno*

Synonyms: *C. florida* 'Alba Plena', *C. florida* 'Flore Pleno', *C.* 'Plena'. Half-hardy, slender, deciduous climber 1.8–2.5 m (6–7.75 ft.) tall. Pruning group 2. Flowering from early summer to early autumn in the garden, and early summer to late autumn under glass. Sumptuous, double, greenish cream long-lasting flowers, 8–10 cm (3.25–4 in.) across,

Clematis florida var. *flore-pleno*. Photo by M. Toomey.

are sterile. Stamens have been modified into layers of numerous petal-like structures, forming the central tight rosette, and are wide at the base and narrowing towards pointed tips. Six outer protective basal tepals, which overlap and taper to points, unfold first to reveal the rosette, and open over a period of days. At the end of the flower's life the layers of petal-like structures drop gradually over a long time too, thereby extending the flowering period. If planted outside, requires moisture-retentive soil in a sheltered, warm location. Best for container culture in a conservatory or cold greenhouse. Zones 7–9.

Clematis florida var. *sieboldiana*. Photo by E. Leeds.

Clematis florida var. sieboldiana

Synonyms: *C. florida* 'Sieboldii, *C. florida* 'Bicolor'. Half-hardy, slender, normally deciduous climber 1.2–2.4 m (3.5–7.75 ft.) tall. If grown under glass, may remain semi-evergreen. Pruning optional, group 2, or group 3. A hard pruning (group 3) delays flowering until midsummer. Flowering from early summer to early autumn in the garden and from early summer to late autumn under glass. Handsome, single, sterile flowers, 8–10 cm (3.25–4 in.) across, consist of six basal overlapping tepals which are creamy white in summer and creamy green in autumn. Superimposed over the tepals is a large central boss of petal-like structures which are purple streaked with white and which stay on the plant for a few days after the main tepals have dropped off. Flowers are held on long stalks with leaf-like bracts halfway between the main stems and flowers. Produced from old and new wood, the flowers look somewhat like passion flowers (*Pas-*

siflora caerulea). Best in a free-draining, moist soil in a warm location. Requires a sheltered position to prevent wind damage to the outer, delicate tepals. Advisable to grow in a container that can be moved to a frost-free site during winter. Looks exceptionally well growing through low to medium-sized shrubs. Excellent for a conservatory. Zones 7–9.

Clematis forsteri

Evergreen Group. Half-hardy, moderately vigorous, evergreen climber or scrambler 2 m (6.5 ft.) tall or taller. Native to New Zealand. Pruning group 1. Flowering from early to midspring. Male and female flowers on separate plants. A cascade of single, creamy lime green, semi-nodding, star-shaped, lemon-scented flowers, 2–3 cm (0.75–1.25 in.) wide, is produced on the previous season's wood. Each flower consists of five to eight tepals. Male plants are recommended because their flowers and leaves are much larger

Clematis forsteri. Photo by M. Toomey.

and more striking than those of female plants. If planted outdoors, best in gritty soil in a sheltered site in sun. Refrain from overwatering. Grow in a container under glass in a conservatory or cold greenhouse to enjoy the scent. Move outdoors during the summer. Zones 8–9.

Clematis 'Foxtrot'

Viticella Group. Hardy, moderately vigorous, deciduous climber 2.4–3 m (7.75–10 ft.) tall. Pruning group 3. Flowering from mid to late summer. Small, single, bluish purple flowers are 7.5–9 cm (3–3.5 in.) wide with four or five broad, spear-shaped tepals. Each tepal has a white centre most prominently at the base and fading towards the tip by way of deep veining. On mature flowers the tepal margins tend to be gently undulating and the tips recurving, giving a blunt appearance. Ideal for a pergola, large trellis, or obelisk. Grow up and over large shrubs and on tall conifers. Zones 4–9.

Clematis 'Foxtrot'. Photo by E. Leeds.

Clematis 'Frances Rivis' (English form)

Atragene Group. RHS Award of Garden Merit (1993). Synonyms: *C. alpina* 'Blue Giant', *C. alpina* 'Francis Rivis', *C. alpina* 'Frances Rives'. Hardy, moderately vigorous, deciduous climber 2.5–3 m (8–10 ft.) tall. Pruning group 1. Flowering from mid to late spring, with a few flowers in late summer. Single, deep sky blue flowers made

Clematis 'Frances Rivis' (English form). Photo by C. Chesshire.

of four tepals, each 6 cm (2.25 in.) long. Best in sharply drained soils. Ideal for north- and east-facing aspects. Excellent for small gardens and patios. Zones 3–9.

Clematis 'Frankie'

Atragene Group. RHS Award of Garden Merit (2002). Synonym: *C. alpina* 'Frankie'. Hardy, moderately vigorous, deciduous climber or scrambler 2.5–3 m (8–10 ft.) tall. Pruning group 1. Flowering from mid to late spring. Single, midblue flowers with four tepals, each 5 cm (2 in.) long and tinged with pale blue at the tip. Best in well-drained soils. Ideal for north- or east-facing aspects. Well suited for small gardens and patios. Zones 3–9.

Clematis 'Freda'

Montana Group. RHS Award of Garden Merit (1993). Half-hardy, moderately vigorous, deciduous climber to 6 m (20 ft.) tall. Pruning group 1. Flowering from late spring to early summer. Single, deep cherry pinkish red flowers 5 cm (2 in.) wide formed of four tepals, each with a paler pink bar down the centre. Attractive bronze leaves turn midgreen with maturity. Best in

Clematis 'Frankie'. Photo by R. Savill.

Clematis 'Freda' hosted by *Pyrus salcifolia* 'Pendula'. Photo by M. Toomey.

sharply drained soils. Suitable for sun or part shade, but produces deepest flower color in full sun. Good for small gardens. Ideal companion for large shrubs with grey foliage. Grow on a pergola or free-standing, large, and sturdy trellis. Zones 7–9.

Clematis 'Fryderyk Chopin'

Hardy, moderately vigorous, compact, deciduous climber 1.2–2.5 m (3.5–8 ft.) tall. Pruning group 2. Profuse flowering over a long period from early

Clematis 'Fryderyk Chopin'. Photo by M. Humphries.

Clematis 'Fujimusume'. Photo by M. Toomey.

to late summer. Single, purple-blue flowers, 10–15 cm (4–6 in.) across, are composed of six oval tepals, which overlap at the base, have irregularly notched and slightly wavy margins, and terminate in gently recurving tips. Suitable for a medium-sized obelisk, free-standing trellis, pole, or post. May be partnered with other not-too-vigorous wall-trained shrubs which do not require annual pruning. Zones 4–9.

Clematis 'Fujimusume'

RHS Award of Garden Merit (2002). A superb cultivar with handsome flowers. Hardy, strong-growing, compact, deciduous climber 2–2.5 m (6.5–8 ft.) tall. Pruning optional, group 2, or group 3. A hard pruning (group 3) results in the loss of early flowers. Flowering from early to mid-summer and again in late summer. Very large, plump flower buds are densely covered with short whitish hairs. The large, single, velvety, light sky blue to purple, flattish flowers are 16–18 cm (6.25–7 in.) across and composed of six to eight smooth tepals which overlap each other slightly and taper towards the tips. The prominent central boss consists of golden yellow stamens. Flowers of the second flush are smaller. Attractive, golden seedheads are well-shaped. Best grown out of direct sunlight in a sheltered site. Suitable for a small obelisk, pillar, or arch. Excellent for container culture. Zones 4–9.

Clematis fusca

Hardy, moderately vigorous, deciduous climber 1–3 m (3–10 ft.) tall. Native to north and northeastern China, Korea, Mongolia, and eastern Russia. Pruning group 3. Flowering from early summer to early autumn. Single, dark purplish brown, nodding or semi-nodding, urn-shaped and rather curious flowers are 2–3 cm (0.75–1.25 in.) long. The four tepals are deeply ribbed, have slightly recurving tips, and are covered in short, woolly, brown hairs. Seedheads are persistent and prominent. Best in well-drained soils. Some shorter forms are self-supporting. Ideal for container culture. Flowers show up well against a light or white background. Zones 3–9.

Clematis fusca. Photo by C. Chesshire.

Clematis 'General Sikorski'. Photo by S. Marczyński.

Clematis 'Gillian Blades'. Photo by E. Leeds.

Clematis 'General Sikorski'

RHS Award of Garden Merit (1993). A floriferous cultivar. Hardy, compact, deciduous climber 1.8–2.4 m (6–7.75 ft.) tall. Pruning group 2. Flowering from early summer to early autumn. Single, mauvish blue, well-rounded flowers, 12–15 cm (4.75–6 in.) wide, are freely produced and consist of six to eight broadly overlapping tepals, each with a hint of pinkish red bar emerging from the base and extending halfway along its length, and with gently notched margins. Best in full or part sun. Train up a pergola, obelisk, or arch. Partner it with wall-trained shrubs which do not require annual pruning. Good specimen plant for container culture. Zones 4–9.

Clematis 'Gillian Blades'

RHS Award of Garden Merit (1993). Hardy, weak-growing, compact, deciduous climber 1.8–2.4 m (6–7.75 ft.) tall. Pruning group 2. Flowering from late spring to midsummer and again in late autumn. Single, pure white flowers are 15–20 cm (6–8 in.) wide and open flat. There are six to eight pointed and gently notched tepals with slightly undulating margins. Early flowers may be tinged with blue. Good against a red brick pillar or wooden post. May be grown in a large container or through low, prostrate conifers or shrubs which do not require annual pruning. Zones 4–9.

Clematis 'Gipsy Queen'

RHS Award of Garden Merit (1993). Hardy, vigorous, deciduous climber 3–3.6 m (10–11.5 ft.) tall. Pruning group 3. Flowering from midsummer to early autumn. Single, velvety, deep violet-purple flowers, 12–14 cm (4.75–5.5 in.) wide, are made of four to six, broad, smooth tepals which are blunt-tipped but narrow at the base, giving

Clematis 'Gipsy Queen'. Photo by C. Chesshire.

Clematis 'Gravetye Beauty'. Photo by J. Pringle.

the flower an open appearance. Partner it with other wall-trained or free-standing shrubs with gold or silvery foliage or with climbing roses. Suitable for a medium-sized to large obelisk, pergola, or arbour. Shows up well against a light background. Zones 4–9.

Clematis 'Gravetye Beauty'

Texensis-Viorna Group. Synonym: *C. texensis* 'Gravetye Beauty'. Hardy, moderately vigorous, deciduous climber 1.8–3 m (6–10 ft.) tall. Normally herbaceous in habit with new shoots emerging from below ground level. Pruning group 3. Flowering from midsummer to midautumn. Single, satiny, rich red flowers are 6–8 cm (2.25–3.25 in.) across and usually face upward. Four to six narrow, pointed tepals, with some incurving margins and slightly recurving tips, are a paler pink on the exterior. When young, the flowers resemble small tulips, but as they mature, the tepals open out—more so than do the tepals of other, similar cultivars. Best flower color in sun or part shade. Prone to mildew. Protect new shoots at soil level from slugs and snails. Train the vines horizontally to enjoy the flowers by looking down into them. Ideal for growing over prostrate conifers, heathers, or a low wall. Zones 4–9.

Clematis 'Guernsey Cream'

An extremely floriferous cultivar. Hardy, not-too-vigorous, compact, deciduous climber 1.8–2.4 m (6–7.75 ft.) tall. Pruning group 2. Flowering from late spring to early summer and again in late summer. Single, creamy white flowers are 12–15 cm (5–6 in.) wide with eight overlapping, pointed tepals. Each tepal has a slightly deeper creamy central bar, which is tinged with green in young flowers. As the flowers mature, the tepals fade to light cream and can look somewhat unsightly. Best in part shade to prevent premature fading of flower color. Ideal against a dark background of prostrate conifers or medium-sized shrubs which do not require annual pruning. Excellent companion for early flowering roses. Train on a small to medium-sized obelisk or trellis. May also be grown in a large container. Zones 4–9.

Clematis 'H. F. Young'

RHS Award of Garden Merit (1993). Hardy, moderately vigorous, deciduous climber 2.4–3 m (7.75–10 ft.) tall. Pruning group 2. Flowering from late spring to early summer and again in early autumn. Large, single, midblue flowers,

Clematis 'Guernsey Cream'. Photo by M. Toomey.

Clematis 'H. F. Young'. Photo by E. Leeds.

Clematis 'Hagley Hybrid'. Photo by M. Toomey.

Clematis 'Hanaguruma'. Photo by C. Chesshire.

15–20 cm (6–8 in.) across, are freely produced. The six to eight overlapping tepals have rounded edges and pointed tips. Reverse of each tepal has a greenish white bar fading into the mauvish blue background. Best in well-drained soil in part shade. Suitable for a pergola, arbour, large trellis, or obelisk. Zones 4–9.

Clematis 'Hagley Hybrid'

Synonym: *C.* 'Pink Chiffon' (in the United States). A very floriferous and popular cultivar. Hardy, not-too-vigorous, compact, deciduous climber 1.8–2.4 m (6–7.75 ft.) tall or slightly taller. Pruning group 3. Flowering from early summer to early autumn. Single, shell-pink flowers are 10–15 cm (4–6 in.) wide and formed of five or six boat-shaped, pointed tepals with crimped edges. Best out of direct sunlight to prevent premature fading of flower color. May be teamed with other low shrubs or roses. Suitable for a low wall or fence. May also be grown in a large container on a terrace, patio, or balcony where it is sheltered from strong winds. Looks well when grown as a groundcover plant. Zones 4–9.

Clematis 'Hanaguruma'

Hardy, moderately vigorous, compact, deciduous climber 1.8–2.4 m (6–7.75 ft.) tall. Pruning group 2. Flowering from late spring to early summer and again in late summer. Single, deep cerise-pink, rounded flowers are 10–15 cm (4–6 in.) across with six to eight broad, overlapping tepals. Each tepal is gently pointed and has textured grooves running along the centres from base to tip. May be partnered with wall-trained shrubs or roses which do not require annual pruning. Suitable for a small obelisk, trellis, or arch. Zones 4–9.

Clematis 'Hanajima'

Herbaceous Integrifolia Group. Hardy, compact, deciduous, low-growing herbaceous perennial to around 30 cm (12 in.) tall. Pruning group 3. Flowering from early to late summer. Single, deep pink, elegant, pendulous, gently ribbed, waxy flowers, 3–4 cm (1.2–1.5 in.) across, are borne initially at the tip of each stem and later from leaf axils. The four tepals are strongly recurving in the upper two thirds and are spreading at the pointed tips. Best in part sun in the front of an herbaceous or mixed border. If an erect-growing plant is wanted, provide the stems with suitable support. May also be grown as a ground cover. Zones 4–9.

Clematis 'Hania'

A relatively new introduction from Poland. Hardy, free-flowering, deciduous climber to 2.5 m (8 ft.) tall. Pruning group 2. Flowering from late spring to midsummer and again from late summer to early autumn. Single, attractive bicolor flowers

Clematis 'Hanajima'. Photo by C. Chesshire.

Clematis 'Hania'. Photo by S. Marczyński.

are deep purplish red with pink margins and measure about 15 cm (6 in.) across. They are composed of six broad, overlapping tepals, each with wavy margins and a distinct white bar on the outside. Early flowers are borne on wood of the previous season, and late flowers are borne on new growths made during the current year. Best in part shade to preserve flower color. Grow as a specimen plant. Team it with medium-size shrubs or roses which do not require annual pruning. Zones 4–9.

Clematis 'Helios'

Tangutica Group. Trade name: Aztek. Synonym: *C. tangutica* 'Helios'. Hardy, moderately vigorous, compact, deciduous climber to 2 m (6.5 ft.) tall or slightly taller. Pruning group 3. Flowering from late spring to early autumn, if left unpruned or

Clematis 'Helios' (Aztek). Photo by M. Toomey.

partially pruned. Single, bright yellow, slightly nodding flowers, 6.5–9 cm (2.5–3.5 in.) wide, are held on long stalks with bright green leaves. The four tepals, each 3.5–4.5 cm (1.25–1.75 in.) long, open quite flat and have pointed tips reflexing like a Turk's cap. The attractive seedheads are persistent. Best in sharply drained soils in sun or part shade. Just right for the small, urban garden. Suitable for short-term container culture or for growing on a free-standing trellis in a mixed border. Grow through medium-sized shrubs with contrasting dark foliage. Zones 4–9.

Clematis 'Helsingborg'

Atragene Group. RHS Award of Garden Merit (1993). Synonym: *C. alpina* 'Helsingborg'. Hardy, moderately vigorous, deciduous climber 2.5–3 m (8–10 ft.) tall or taller. Pruning group 1. Once the plant is well established, remove a few old vines each year immediately after flowering to keep it tidy. Flowering from mid to late spring. Single, blue-purple flowers have an inner skirt of pale purple petal-like structures, similar in color to the reverse side of the tepals. Four slightly twisted tepals, each 5 cm (2 in.) long, are slightly paler at the margins. Best in sharply drained soils. Suitable for any aspect, including cold ones. Ideal for small gardens. Team it with another robust shrub which does not need annual pruning or grow it as a specimen plant on a sturdy trellis. Zones 3–9.

Clematis 'Hendersonii'

Herbaceous/Integrifolia Group. RHS Award of Merit (1965). Synonyms: *C. integrifolia* 'Hendersonii', *C. integrifolia* 'Henderson'. Hardy, deciduous, non-climbing plant with herbaceous stems 0.6–0.9 m (2–3 ft.) tall. Pruning group 3. Flowering from mid to late summer. Single, deep midblue, bell-shaped, slightly scented, solitary flowers with

Clematis 'Helsingborg'. Photo by J. Lindmark.

Clematis 'Hendersonii'. Photo by J. Lindmark.

Clematis 'Henryi'. Photo by E. Leeds.

four pointed tepals, each 5.5–6.5 cm (2.25–2.5 in.) long with slightly undulating margins. With age the tepals twist in different directions. Outer side of the tepals has prominent darker colored ridges starting at the base and receding towards the tip. Suitable for any aspect but produces strongest scent in a sunny position. Furnish the plant with a suitable support and tie-in the stems, or let it scramble through other plants in an herbaceous or mixed border. Zones 3–9.

Clematis 'Henryi'

RHS Award of Merit (1873), RHS Award of Garden Merit (1993). Synonym: *C.* 'Bangholm Belle'. A very old, popular plant which may take time to settle down and grow well. Hardy, vigorous, deciduous climber 3–3.6 m (10–11.5 ft.) tall. Very floriferous when established. Pruning group 2. Flowering from late spring to late summer. Single, satiny white flowers, 15–20 cm (6–8 in.) wide, are composed of six to eight, smooth, overlapping, pointed tepals, each with a pale green bar on the outside. Thrives in well-drained garden soils enriched with humus. Best in a sheltered, warm site. Shows up well against a dark background. Suitable as a specimen plant supported by an obelisk, trellis, or pergola. May be grown with other shrubs or roses which do not require annual pruning. Zones 4–9.

Clematis heracleifolia

Herbaceous/Heracleifolia Group. RHS Award of Merit (1962). Hardy, woody-based, deciduous, semi-herbaceous subshrub 0.6–0.9 m (2–3 ft.) tall. Native to central and eastern China. Pruning group 3. Flowering from early summer to early autumn. Male and female flowers are separate but borne on the same plant. Small, single, deep blue or purple-blue, nodding or partly nodding, tubular flowers, 1.5–2 cm (0.5–0.75 in.) across, are hyacinth-shaped and somewhat hairy on the outside. The four tepals, each 1.5–3 cm (0.5–1.25 in.) long, recurve at the expanded, blunt, frilled tip as the flower matures. Best in free-draining but moist garden soils. Plant in an herbaceous or mixed border or grow as a specimen plant in a very large container. Zones 5–9.

Clematis 'Honora'

Hardy, moderately vigorous, deciduous climber 3–4 m (10–13 ft.) tall with somewhat hairy stems. Pruning optional, group 2, or group 3. A hard pruning (group 3) results in the loss of early flowers. Flowering from early summer to early autumn. Single, rich violet-purple, solitary flowers, 18 cm (7 in.) across, are borne freely. Six long-pointed tepals are shaded with burgundy and have small

Clematis heracleifolia. Photo by C. Chesshire.

Clematis 'Honora'. Photo by C. Chesshire.

Clematis 'Horn of Plenty'. Photo by C. Chesshire.

gaps between them at the base. A deeper purple central bar runs from the base to the tip of each tepal. Margins of tepals are wavy. As the flower matures, the tepals twist and bend backwards. Suitable for a medium-sized obelisk, arch, or trellis. If group 3 pruning is utilized, grow naturally through shrubs, roses, or conifers. Zones 4–9.

Clematis 'Horn of Plenty'

RHS Award of Garden Merit (1993). Hardy, moderately vigorous, deciduous climber 2–3 m (6.5–10 ft.) tall. Pruning optional, group 2, or group 3. A hard pruning (group 3) results in loss of early flowers. Flowering from late spring to early summer and again in late summer. Large, single, rosy mauve, cup-shaped flowers are 15–20 cm (6–8 in.) wide with six to eight overlapping, blunt-tipped tepals. Each tepal has a deeper colored central bar with veining and slightly notched margins. Best on an obelisk, trellis, or pergola if no pruning or light pruning (group 2) is undertaken. Zones 4–9.

Clematis 'Huldine'

RHS Award of Merit (1934), RHS Award of Garden Merit (2002). A very old, fine, floriferous cultivar. Hardy, vigorous, strong-growing, deciduous climber 3–4.6 m (10–15 ft.) tall or taller. Pruning group 3. For early flowers, retain a few old stems. Flowering from mid to late summer. Small, single, pearly white, cup-shaped flowers, 7.5–10 cm (3–4 in.) wide, are borne in abundance and consist of six translucent tepals which do not overlap. Each tepal boasts three pinkish mauve central bars on the undersurface and has slightly incurved margins and a recurved tip. Suitable in full sun or part shade. Ideal for a large trellis, arch, or pergola. Best where the undersurface of the flowers can be viewed with ease. May also be teamed with medium-sized trees or large shrubs. Zones 4–9.

Clematis 'Huldine'. Photo by J. Lindmark.

Clematis 'Huvi'

Hardy, moderately vigorous, compact, deciduous climber 1.8–2.4 m (6–7.75 ft.) tall. Pruning group 2. Flowering from early to late summer. Single, deep carmine red flowers are 12–14 cm (4.75–5.5 in.) across with six boat-shaped tepals, each with incurving wavy margins at the base, becoming reflexed towards the tip. The central rib of the tepal has a reddish mauve color between the grooving which runs from base to tip. Best in garden soils enriched with humus. Ideal for container culture. Train on an obelisk or trellis. Zones 3–9.

Clematis 'Huvi'. Photo by E. Leeds.

Clematis ianthina var. ianthina

Synonym: *C. fusca* var. *violacea*. Hardy, not-too-vigorous, deciduous climber 1.8–2.4 m (6–7.75 ft) tall. Native to China, Korea, and eastern Russia. Pruning group 3. Flowering from early to late summer. Small, single, blue-violet to purple, nodding to semi-nodding, urn-shaped flowers are 2–3 cm (0.75–1.25 in.) long. Four ribbed tepals recurve at their tips and expose purple-blue insides. Seedheads are large. Best in sharply drained soils. Shows up well against a light or white background. Ideal for container culture. Zones 3–9.

Clematis ianthina var. *ianthina*. Photo by C. Chesshire.

Clematis integrifolia. Photo by J. Lindmark.

Clematis integrifolia

Herbaceous/Integrifolia Group. A very old species. Hardy, deciduous, non-clinging, clump-forming woody-based subshrub or herbaceous perennial 0.6–0.9 m (2–3 ft.) tall. Native to central and eastern Europe. Pruning group 3. Flowering from early summer to early autumn. Single, mauvish blue to deep blue, solitary, nodding, bell-shaped flowers, 3–5 cm (1.25–2 in.) long, are borne on long stalks terminally or laterally at the uppermost leaf joints. The four pointed, half-spreading, and recurving tepals are invariably twisted. Attractive seedheads have shiny, silvery, and feathery seed-tails. Slender, ribbed stems rise from the ground annually. Splendid for the front half of an herbaceous or mixed border. Provide suitable supports to prevent the stems from flopping around too much. Zones 4–9.

Clematis 'Ivan Olsson'. Photo by C. Chesshire.

Clematis 'Ivan Olsson'

Hardy, not-too-vigorous, compact, deciduous climber 1.8–2.4 m (6–7.75 ft.) tall. Pruning group 2. Flowering from late spring to early summer

Clematis 'Jackmanii'. Photo by J. Lindmark.

and again in late summer. Ice-blue flowers are 8–14 cm (3.25–5.5 in.) wide with deeper blue margins. Single flowers are composed of six to eight tepals, semi-double flowers have a dozen tepals. Ideal for container culture. Suitable for a short trellis or small obelisk, or allow to grow through low shrubs which do not require annual pruning. Zones 4–9.

Clematis 'Jackmanii'

RHS First Class Certificate (1863), RHS Award of Garden Merit (1993). A very old, widely grown, universally popular, and free-flowering cultivar. Hardy, vigorous, deciduous climber 3–3.6 m (10–11.5 ft.) tall or taller. Pruning group 3. Flowering from early to late summer. Single, velvety, dark purple, gently semi-nodding, gappy flowers are 10 cm (4 in.) wide. The four to six

tepals are broad, slightly twisted, blunt, and rough-textured, each with reddish purple grooves along its centre. Makes an ideal specimen plant on a trellis, obelisk, or pergola. Grow up and over large shrubs and small trees. Zones 3–9.

Clematis 'Jackmanii Alba'

Hardy, vigorous, deciduous climber 3–3.6 m (10–11.5 ft.) tall or taller. Pruning optional, group 2, or group 3. For early flowers, do not prune back to the previous year's wood. Flowering from early to midsummer and again in late summer. Double, light bluish mauve flowers, 12.5 cm (5 in.) wide, are borne on old wood of the previous season and composed of many layers of textured, pointed tepals which are of uneven lengths. Color fades to white with age. Some tepals may

Clematis 'Jackmanii Alba'. Photo by E. Leeds.

Clematis 'Jackmanii Rubra' early flowers are usually semi-double. Photo by J. Lindmark.

Clematis 'Jackmanii Superba'. Photo by C. Chesshire.

be tinged with green, and on the reverse of each one is a greenish bar. Single flowers consist of six white tepals and are produced on the current year's new growth. Best in full or part sun. Suitable for a large trellis, obelisk, arbour, or pergola. Grow up and over or through small trees and large shrubs which do not require regular pruning. Zones 4–9.

Clematis 'Jackmanii Rubra'

Hardy, strong-growing, deciduous climber 3–3.6 m (10–11.5 ft.) tall or taller. Pruning group 2. Flowering during early summer and again in late summer. Double and semi-double, crimson flowers, borne on old wood of the previous season, are 12.5 cm (5 in.) wide, tinged purplish red, and composed of six tapering tepals, upon which are arranged more layers of shorter tepals. Single flowers with four to six tepals are produced later in the season on the current year's new growth. Suitable for a pergola, arbour, medium-sized to large obelisk, or trellis. Grow with other wall-trained plants or through large shrubs which do not require major pruning. Zones 4–9.

Clematis 'Jackmanii Superba'

Hardy vigorous, deciduous climber 3–3.6 m (10–11.5 ft.) tall. Pruning group 3. Flowering from early to late summer. Single, velvety, dark violet-mauve flowers are 13–14 cm (5–5.5 in.) wide and formed of four to six tepals which are broader but otherwise similar in shape to those of *C.* 'Jackmanii'. Each tepal has a deeper reddish purple flush down the middle that fades as the flower matures. Ideal for a trellis, pergola, or obelisk. Grow through medium-sized trees, especially fruit trees, to give late summer interest. Peg out in island beds and use as ground cover. Zones 3–9.

Clematis 'Jacqueline du Pré'

Atragene Group. RHS Award of Garden Merit (2002). Synonym: *C. alpina* 'Jacqueline du Pré'. Hardy, moderately vigorous, deciduous climber 2.4–3 m (7.75–10 ft.) tall. Pruning group 1. Flowering from early to midspring. Small, single, rosy mauvish pink, bell-shaped, nodding flowers are made of four broad, tapering tepals, each 6.3 cm (2.5 in.) long, with darker shaded veins running from base to tip and wavy, silver-pink margins.

Clematis 'Jacqueline du Pré'. Photo by C. Chesshire.

Tepals are paler colored inside and surround an inner skirt of spoon-shaped, pale pink staminodes. Best in well-drained garden soils enriched with humus. Ideal for colder parts of the garden. Grow on an obelisk, pergola, or trellis. Zones 3–9.

Clematis 'James Mason'

Hardy, moderately vigorous, deciduous climber 1.8–2.4 m (6–7.75 ft.) tall. Pruning group 2. Flowering from late spring to early summer and again in late summer. Large, single, white flowers are 15–20 cm (6–8 in.) wide. Eight overlapping tepals taper to fine points and have undulating margins. Each tepal has three deep grooves along the centre. Requires a sheltered position to prevent wind damage to the flowers. Ideal for container culture. Suitable for a medium-sized obelisk. Zones 4–9.

Clematis 'James Mason'. Photo by C. Chesshire.

Clematis 'Jan Lindmark'. Photo by J. Lindmark.

Clematis 'Jan Lindmark'

Atragene Group. Synonym: *C. macropetala* 'Jan Lindmark'. Hardy, moderately vigorous, compact, deciduous climber 2–2.5 m (6.5–8 ft.) tall. Pruning group 1. Flowering from early to late spring. Single, purple-mauve flowers consist of four tepals, each with darker streaks and measuring 3.5 cm (1.25 in.) long. The tepals open out to reveal an inner skirt of petal-like staminodes, which are paler in color and are twisted and kinked in form, giving a spidery appearance to the whole flower. Best in well-drained garden soils enriched with humus. Suitable for any aspect, even a cold one. Shows up well against a white or light background. Ideal for a small garden or container culture. Zones 3–9.

Clematis 'Jan Pawel II'

Synonym: *C.* 'John Paul II'. Hardy, vigorous, deciduous climber 2.5–3 m (8–10 ft.) tall. Pruning group 2 or 3. A hard pruning (group 3) delays flowering. Flowering from mid to late summer. Single, creamy white flowers, 13–14 cm (5–5.5

Clematis 'Jan Pawel II'. Photo by S. Marczyński.

in.) wide, have pink trails which become more prominent in late summer as a pink bar. There are six firm, broad, creased, overlapping, and pointed tepals. Best in part shade to preserve flower color. Suitable for an obelisk, trellis, or pergola. If using pruning group 3, grow naturally through shrubs with dark foliage. Zones 4–9.

Clematis 'John Warren'. Photo by R. Surman.

Clematis 'John Huxtable'

RHS Award of Garden Merit (2002). Hardy, moderately vigorous, compact, deciduous climber 2.5–3 m (8–10 ft.) tall. Pruning group 3. Flowering from mid to late summer. Single, translucent, creamy white flowers are 11–12 cm (4.5–4.75 in.) across and composed of six tapering, textured tepals with slightly recurving tips. Team it with climbing roses and other wall-trained shrubs with dark foliage. Suitable for a trellis, obelisk, or small arch. Zones 4–9.

Clematis 'John Warren'

Hardy, moderately vigorous, compact, deciduous climber 2.5–3 m (8–10 ft.) tall. Pruning group 2. Flowering from late spring to early summer and again in late summer. Large, single, pinky grey flowers, 20–23 cm (8–9 in.) across, consist of six to eight overlapping, pointed tepals, each overlaid with a deeper pink stripe along the middle. Tepal margins are richly colored but fading with age. Best in part shade. Requires a sheltered posi-

Clematis 'John Huxtable'. Photo by C. Chesshire.

tion to prevent wind damage to the large flowers. Ideal for a trellis, obelisk, or pergola. May be grown through a medium-sized shrub which does not require severe annual pruning. Zones 4–9.

Clematis 'Julka'

Silver medal winner at the Plantarium 2002 Arboricultural Trade Fair. A Polish cultivar. Hardy deciduous climber up to 2.5 m (8 ft.) tall. New growths are purplish. Pruning group 1. Flowering from early to midsummer. Large, single, velvety violet flowers, about 15 cm (6 in.) across, are borne freely. Each of the six tepals has a deep purple-red bar. Best in part or full shade. Suitable

for an arch, pergola, trellis, or other garden support. May be partnered with small trees, conifers, or shrubs. Recommended for small gardens. Zones 5–9.

Clematis 'Juuli'

Herbaceous/Integrifolia Group. A very floriferous cultivar. Hardy, non-clinging, herbaceous shrub 1.2–1.5 m (3.5–5 ft.) tall. Pruning group 3. Flowering from mid to late summer. Small, single, purplish blue flowers, 7.5–9 cm (3–3.5 in.) across, are outward-facing and borne in great profusion on the current season's new growth. The five or six spoon-shaped tepals do not overlap. Each

Clematis 'Julka'. Photo by S. Marczyński.

Clematis 'Juuli'. Photo by J. Lindmark.

Clematis 'Kacper' (Caspar). Photo by C. Chesshire.

Clematis 'Kaiu'. Photo by C. Chesshire.

tepal has a prominent central groove tinged pinkish purple. Tepal margins fade to pale blue with age, leaving a more prominent central rib. Best in garden soils enriched with humus. Ideal underplanted in a rose bed where it can be left to scramble at will. Grow in a container where it can overflow or allow it to tumble over a low wall, shrub, or prostrate conifer. Zones 3–9.

Clematis 'Kacper'

Trade name: Caspar. Hardy, moderately vigorous, deciduous climber 1.8–2.4 m (6–7.75 ft.) tall or taller. Pruning group 2. Flowering from late spring to early summer and again in late summer. Large, single, intense violet-blue flowers, 20–23 cm (8–9 in.) wide, are made of six to eight broad, overlapping tepals with finely scalloped margins. Tepal color is deeper along the middle. Best in part shade. Requires a sheltered position to prevent wind damage to the large flowers. Shows up well against a light background. Suitable for a pergola, obelisk, or trellis. May be partnered with other clematis in pruning group 2. Zones 4–9.

Clematis 'Kaiu'

Texensis-Viorna Group. Hardy, compact, herbaceous climber 1.5–1.8 m (5–6 ft.) tall. Pruning group 3. Flowering from mid to late summer. Single, greyish white, pitcher-shaped, nodding flowers are 3–4 cm (1.25–1.5 in.) long. The four tepals are tinged with pale purple or pink when young, becoming whiter with age. The pointed tips of the tepals gently curving outwards and upwards. Ideal for large containers or for growing on a medium-sized obelisk. Allow the plant to grow naturally and freely. Refrain from tying-in the stems tightly to a support. Partner it with a robust, climbing or shrub rose. Zones 3–9.

Clematis 'Kakio'

Trade name: Pink Champagne. Hardy, moderately vigorous, compact, deciduous climber 1.8–2.4 m (6–7.75 ft.) tall. Pruning group 2. Flowering from late spring to early summer on the previous season's growth and again in summer on the current year's growth. Single, purple-

Clematis 'Kakio' (Pink Champagne). Photo by E. Leeds.

Clematis 'Kardynal Wyszyński' (Cardinal Wyszynski). Photo by S. Marczyński.

red or deep pink flowers, 14–16.5 cm (5.5–6.5 in.) wide, are borne in masses and are composed of six to eight overlapping, pointed tepals, which are deepest pink at the margins, fading to a central mauvish bar covered with pink veins. Suitable for short-term container culture. Grow on a small to medium-sized obelisk or trellis, or through other not-too-vigorous, wall-trained climbers which do not require severe pruning. Zones 4–9.

Clematis 'Kardynal Wyszyński'

Trade name: Cardinal Wyszynski. Hardy, very vigorous, deciduous climber 2.5–3.6 m (8–11.5 ft.) tall or taller. Pruning group 3. Flowering from early to late summer. Single, glowing crimson flowers 15–20 cm (6–8 in.) across with six to eight overlapping, pointed tepals. Best in a sheltered spot with a modicum of sunshine. Ideal for a pergola, obelisk, or trellis. Zones 4–9.

Clematis 'Kasmu'

Viticella Group. Synonym: *C. viticella* 'Signe'. Hardy, moderately vigorous, deciduous climber 2.5–3 m (8–10 ft.) tall. Pruning group 3. Flowering from mid to late summer. Single, velvety, deep violet-pink flowers, 10–15 cm (4–6 in.) across, are composed of four to six tepals, each with light purple veins and a pronounced white stripe. Best in a bright, sunny site. Shows up well against a light background. Use in natural planting with other shrubs and prostrate conifers. Suitable for a pergola, trellis, or obelisk. Zones 4–9.

Clematis 'Kasugayama'

Hardy, moderately vigorous, compact, deciduous climber 1.8–2.4 m (6–7.75 ft.) tall. Pruning group 2. Flowering from late spring to early summer and again during late summer. Single, bright lavender-blue flowers are 6–8 cm (2.25–3.25 in.)

Clematis 'Kasmu'. Photo by R. Savill.

Clematis 'Kasugayama'. Photo by C. Chesshire.

Clematis 'Ken Donson'. Photo by C. Chesshire.

Clematis 'Kiri Te Kanawa'. Photo by C. Chesshire.

wide with six to eight tepals. Ideal for container culture. May be grown on a small obelisk or short trellis. Zones 4–9.

Clematis 'Ken Donson'

RHS Award of Garden Merit (1993). A fine all-around cultivar noted for its flowers, seedheads, beautiful leaves, and long flowering period. Hardy, not-too-vigorous, deciduous climber 2.5–3 m (8–10 ft.) tall. Pruning group 2. Flowering from early summer to early autumn. Single, purplish deep blue flowers, 15–18 cm (6–7 in.) wide, are well-formed and composed of six, broad but pointed tepals, each with a whitish bar on the reverse that fades into blue at the margins. Ideal for a medium-sized trellis or obelisk. May be grown with other wall-trained shrubs which do not require annual pruning. Zones 4–9.

Clematis 'Kermesina'

Viticella Group. RHS Award of Garden Merit (2002). Synonyms: *C. viticella* 'Kermesina', *C. viticella* 'Rubra'. A very floriferous cultivar. Hardy, vigorous, deciduous climber 3–4 m (10–13 ft.) tall. Pruning group 3. Flowering from midsummer to early autumn. Single, deep crimson, semi-nodding flowers, 6 cm (2.25 in.) across, are usually composed of four blunt tepals, each with recurving margins and a white blotch at the base. The tepals surround greenish filaments and almost black anthers. Early in the season, the tips of the tepals may have green markings. Shows up well against a light background. Ideal for growing through medium-sized trees, conifers, and large shrubs, or as a specimen plant on a free-standing obelisk, trellis, or pergola. Zones 3–9.

Clematis 'Kiri Te Kanawa'

Hardy, compact, deciduous climber 1.8–2.4 m (6–7.75 ft.) tall. Pruning group 2. Flowering from late spring to early summer and again in late summer. Sumptuous, double, deep purplish blue flowers, 12.5–15 cm (5–6 in.) wide, are formed of many layers of broad yet pointed, overlapping tepals. The flowers, which are produced on the previous season's old wood and the current season's new growth, tend to get smaller as the

NO POSTAGE
NECESSARY
IF MAILED
IN THE
UNITED STATES

BUSINESS REPLY MAIL
FIRST CLASS MAIL PERMIT NO. 717 PORTLAND, OR

POSTAGE WILL BE PAID BY ADDRESSEE

TIMBER PRESS, INC.
The Haseltine Building
133 S.W. Second Avenue, Suite 450
Portland, OR 97204-9743

TIMBER PRESS

Thank you for choosing this Timber Press book. Our books are widely available at good bookstores and garden centers.

To receive our free catalog or e-mail announcements, complete and return this card, or visit our Web site at: **www.timberpress.com/rr**

Name (please print)

Address

City _____ State _____ Zip _____

E-mail address

☐ I prefer not to receive e-mail announcements.
☐ Do not share this information with any other company or organization.

We'd also welcome your comments on this book.

Title of book: _____

Comments: _____

Please check your areas of interest:

☐ Annuals (45AN)
☐ Architecture (45AC)
☐ Art of Plants (45AR)
☐ Bonsai/Penjing (45BO)
☐ Botany (4400)
☐ Bulbs (45BU)
☐ Cacti/Succulents (45CA)
☐ Climbers/Vines (45CL)
☐ Ethnobotany (44ET)
☐ Grasses & Groundcover (45GA)
☐ Growers/Professional (45GR)
☐ Herbs (45HE)
☐ Landscaping & Design (45LA)
☐ Literature (45LT)

☐ Low-Water Gardening (45LW)
☐ Mosses, Ferns & Fungi (45MO)
☐ Native Plants (45NP)
☐ Natural History (45NH)
☐ Natural Resource Mgmt. (4800)
☐ NW Regional (4100)
☐ Orchids (45OR)
☐ Perennials (45PE)
☐ Regional (45RE)
☐ Rhododendrons/Azaleas (45RH)
☐ Rock Gardening (45RG)
☐ Roses (45RO)
☐ Trees & Shrubs (45TR)
☐ Tropicals & Exotics (45TO)

Clematis 'Kermesina'. Photo by J. Lindmark.

season progresses. Best in full sun or part shade. Requires a sheltered position to prevent wind damage to the flowers. Grow on a small to medium-sized obelisk or trellis, or with medium-sized shrubs which have softly colored foliage and similar pruning requirements. Ideal for container culture. Zones 4–9.

Clematis 'Kirimäe'

Hardy, moderately vigorous, compact, deciduous climber 1.8–2.4 m (6–7.75 ft.) tall. Pruning group 2. Flowering from late spring to early summer and again in late summer. Single, very light pink flowers are 10–12 cm (4–4.75 in.) across and made of six tepals, each with a reddish pink bar. Best in part shade to prevent premature fading of flower color. Ideal for container culture. Suitable for a small obelisk or trellis. Zones 4–9.

Clematis 'Kommerei'

A splendid newer cultivar from Estonia. Hardy, not-too-vigorous, free-flowering, deciduous climber 1.8–3.5 m (6–11 ft.) tall. Pruning group 3. Flowering from late summer to early autumn. Large, single, reddish purple, solitary flowers, 8–14 cm (3.5–5.5 in.) across, are borne in leaf axils. The four to six overlapping tepals have wavy margins and taper to blunt tips. Best in semi-shade to shade to retain the rich flower color. Suitable for a pergola, obelisk, or free-standing trellis. May be grown through large shrubs or roses with medium vigour, although makes a handsome display when grown as a specimen plant. Zones 4–9.

Clematis 'Königskind'

Hardy, very compact, deciduous climber 1.2–1.8 m (3.5–6 ft.) tall. Pruning group 2. Flowering from late spring to early summer and again in late summer. Single, mauvish blue, upward-facing flowers are 10–12 cm (4–4.75 in.) wide with six to eight broad yet pointed, overlapping tepals. Suitable for container culture. May be trained on a trellis or other suitable supports. Zones 4–9.

Clematis 'Kirimäe'. Photo by R. Savill.

Clematis 'Kommerei'. Photo by E. Leeds.

Clematis 'Königskind'. Photo by J. Lindmark.

Clematis 'Kugotia' (Golden Tiara). Photo by E. Leeds.

Clematis 'Lady Betty Balfour'. Photo by J. Lindmark.

Clematis 'Kugotia'

Tangutica Group. RHS Award of Garden Merit (2002), British Clematis Society Certificate of Merit (1999). Trade names: Golden Tiara, Tiara Gold. Hardy, compact, not-too-vigorous, deciduous climber 2–3 m (6.5–10 ft.) tall. Pruning group 3. Flowering from midsummer to early autumn, with main display from late summer to early autumn. Single, bright yellow to orange-yellow, nodding, lemon-scented flowers, 5–7 cm (2–2.75 in.) across, are at first broadly bell-shaped, later becoming more open. The four thick tepals have tips which turn upwards and margins which turn slightly back on themselves. A prominent central boss of dark mauvish brown stamens contrasts well with the tepal color. Seedheads are persistent. Best in well-drained garden soils. Suitable for a pergola, obelisk, or freestanding trellis. May be grown through large shrubs with dark foliage. Zones 4–9.

Clematis 'Lady Betty Balfour'

RHS Award of Merit (1912). Hardy, very vigorous, deciduous climber 3–3.6 m (10–11.5 ft.) tall. Throws up numerous new shoots annually. Pruning group 3. Flowering from late summer to late autumn. Single, deep, rich blue flowers are 15–20 cm (6–8 in.) wide and composed of six broad, overlapping tepals surrounding a central boss of contrasting creamy yellow stamens. Young tepals tend to boast a dash of red near the base; this red disappears with age. Best in full sun since it flowers late. Allow to grow naturally through robust, medium-sized shrubs, trees, and conifers, especially those with light foliage. Suitable for a trellis, arbour, arch, or pergola. Zones 4–9.

Clematis 'Lady Bird Johnson'. Photo by C. Chesshire.

Clematis 'Lady Bird Johnson'

Texensis-Viorna Group. Synonym: *C. texensis* 'Lady Bird Johnson'. Hardy, deciduous, slender climber 2.5–3 m (8–10 ft.) tall. Normally herbaceous in habit with new shoots emerging from below ground level. Pruning group 3. Flowering from midsummer to early autumn. Single, dusky red, tulip-like flowers are 4–5 cm (1.5–2 in.) across with four tepals which recurve on maturity. Each tepal has a slightly brighter crimson central bar. Best in full sun or part shade. Prone to mildew. Protect new shoots at soil level from slugs and snails. Partner it with climbing roses. Flowers look exceptionally well when grown over prostrate conifers, low-growing shrubs, and other groundcover plants. Zones 4–9.

Clematis 'Lady Caroline Nevill'

Hardy, moderately vigorous, deciduous climber 2.4–3 m (7.75–10 ft.) tall. Flowering from early to midsummer and again in late summer. Flowers of the first flush, produced on wood made the previous year, are semi-double and 12.5–15 cm (5–6 in.) across. They are composed of a basal

Clematis 'Lady Caroline Nevill'. Photo by C. Chesshire.

layer of pale whitish mauve tepals, each with a deeper mauve bar running from the base to the tip. This layer of tepals is overlaid with a varying number of narrower, shorter tepals. A second flush of flowers is produced on the current season's new growth later in the summer. These flowers are single, smaller, and paler in color and are composed of overlapping, pointed tepals. Best in full or part sun. Suitable for a pergola, trellis, or obelisk. Zones 4–9.

Clematis 'Lady Londesborough'

RHS First Class Certificate (1869). Hardy, not-too-vigorous, compact, deciduous climber 1.8–2.4 m (6–7.75 ft.) tall. Flowering from late spring to early summer and again in midsummer. Small, single, satiny, pale pinkish mauve flowers are

12.5–15 cm (5–6 in.) wide and fade to silver mauve with age. Each of the eight overlapping tepals has slightly notched or wavy margins and a hint of a pale mauve central bar. Best in a warm, sheltered site. Shows up well against a dark background. Suitable for an arch, small pergola, or obelisk. Grow with other wall-trained, moderately vigorous shrubs and small to medium-sized roses. Good for a large container. Zones 4–9.

Clematis 'Lady Northcliffe'

RHS Award of Merit (1906). Hardy, very vigorous but compact, deciduous climber 1.8–2.4 m (6–7.75 ft.) tall. Flowering from early summer to early autumn. Small, single, deep royal blue flowers, 13–15 cm (5–6 in.) across, fade to lavender-

Clematis 'Lady Londesborough'. Photo by R. Surman.

Clematis 'Lady Northcliffe'. Photo by J. Lindmark.

blue with age. The six to eight more or less half-upright tepals do not lie flat and are broad, overlapping, and pointed. Edges of tepals are wavy and gently notched. Best in a warm, sheltered position. Suitable for a pergola, trellis, or small obelisk and for container culture. Partner it with shrubs which do not require annual pruning. Zones 4–9.

Clematis 'Lambton Park'

Tangutica Group. RHS Award of Garden Merit (2002). Synonym: *C. tangutica* 'Lambton Park'. Hardy, moderately vigorous, deciduous climber 3–4 m (10–13 ft.) tall or taller. Pruning group 3. Flowering over a long period from early summer to midautumn. Single, bright buttercup yellow, nodding flowers are lantern-like with four broad, pointed tepals, each 5 cm (2 in.) long, with a thick margin recurving to expose prominent yellowish green anthers. Currently the largest flowers of any cultivar of *Clematis tangutica*. Some clones exude a coconut scent. Large, silky seedheads develop as the earlier flowers wither and are carried on the plant as the flowering continues. Best in well-drained garden soils. Superb on a pergola or free-standing trellis. Allow to grow through large shrubs or medium-sized trees. Zones 4–9.

Clematis 'Lasurstern'

RHS Award of Garden Merit (1993). An old, much-loved cultivar with a long flowering period. Hardy, strong-growing, deciduous climber 2.5–3 m (8–10 ft.) tall. Flowering from late spring to early summer and again in late summer. Large, single, deep lavender-blue flowers, 18–23 cm (7–9 in.) wide, open out fully and lie flat. Six to eight tepals with undulating edges overlap at the base and smartly taper to acute points. With age, color tends to fade along the centre of each tepal, but the flowers, whose large size and shape almost hide the leaves, are held well on the plant for a long time. Flowers are produced from the previous season's old wood. The large, spherical seedheads are useful in flower arrangements. Requires a sheltered position to prevent wind damage to the flowers. Suitable for growing on a trellis, obelisk, or arch. Zones 4–9.

Clematis 'Lambton Park'. Photo by J. Lindmark.

Clematis 'Lasurstern'. Photo by E. Leeds.

Clematis 'Lawsoniana'

Hardy, moderately vigorous, compact, deciduous climber 2.5–3 m (8–10 ft.) tall. Flowering from early summer to early autumn. Single, mauvish blue flowers 18–23 cm (7–9 in.) across are held well at the ends of long stalks and produced over a long period. Six to eight tepals overlap and taper towards the tips. A hint of pink is very noticeable as the young flowers open, and with age the general color fades to pale lavender-blue. Requires a sheltered position to prevent wind damage to the large flowers. Suitable for a trellis or pergola. May be teamed with a low-growing shrub which does not require annual pruning. Zones 4–9.

Clematis 'Lawsoniana'. Photo by J. Lindmark.

Clematis 'Lemon Chiffon'. Photo by M. Toomey.

Clematis 'Lemon Chiffon'

Synonym: *C.* 'Yellow Chiffon'. Shy to flower—be patient. Hardy, not-too-vigorous, compact, deciduous climber 1.8–2.4 m (6–7.75 ft.) tall. Pruning group 2. Flowering from late spring to early summer and again in late summer. Large, single, pale yellow-cream flowers are 10–15 cm (4–6 in.) wide with eight rounded, wide, overlapping, slightly recurving tepals. Seedheads are large. Best in part shade to prevent premature fading of flower color. Shows up well against a dark background. Suitable for a small obelisk or trellis. Useful for container culture. May be teamed with a low-growing shrub which does not require annual pruning. Zones 4–9.

Clematis ligusticifolia
Western virgin's bower

Vitalba Group. Not for gardens with limited space. Hardy, vigorous, deciduous climber 4–7 m (13–23 ft.) tall or taller. Native to southwestern Canada, western United States, and northern Mexico. Not very floriferous in British gardens. Pruning group 3. Flowering from midsummer to early autumn. Single, white flowers with long, slender stalks are borne in loose clusters along the upper lengths of the stems. The four narrow, egg-shaped tepals, each 1.3 cm (0.5 in.) long, are widely spread apart and are covered with fine soft hairs on both surfaces. The ridged stems are often shaded dark purple

Clematis ligusticifolia. Photo by J. Lindmark.

Clematis 'Lincoln Star'. Photo by C. Chesshire.

on mature vines and become woody with age. Best in well-drained garden soils in sun or part shade. Very drought tolerant. Useful for clothing a very large tree, wall, robust fence, or sturdy pergola. Zones 5–9.

Clematis 'Lincoln Star'

Hardy, moderately vigorous, deciduous climber 2.4–3 m (7.75–10 ft.) tall. Pruning group 2. Flowering from late spring to early summer and again in late summer. Single, raspberry pink, gappy flowers are 15 cm (6 in.) wide with six to eight pointed tepals, each with a deeper pink central bar. Best in part shade to prevent premature fading of flower color. Shows up well against a dark background. Ideal for a pergola, small arch, or trellis. Zones 4–9.

Clematis 'Little Nell'

Viticella Group. Synonym: *C. viticella* 'Little Nell'. A very floriferous cultivar. Hardy, moderately vigorous, deciduous climber 2.5–3 m (8–10 ft.) tall. Pruning group 3. Flowering from midsummer to early autumn. Single, pale creamy white, semi-nodding flowers are 5–6.5 cm (2–2.5 in.) across, with mauvish pink margins. The four or five tepals have distinct mauvish pink veins and are gently recurved at the somewhat broad tips. Grow through small to medium-sized trees and large shrubs. Zones 3–9.

Clematis 'Lord Herschell'

Herbaceous Group. Hardy, deciduous, non-clinging plant with herbaceous stems 46–61 cm (18–24 in.) tall. Pruning group 3. Flowering from

Clematis 'Little Nell'. Photo by J. Lindmark.

Clematis 'Lord Herschell'. Photo by E. Leeds.

late spring to late summer. Single, rich, velvety reddish purple, tulip-shaped flowers are 5 cm (2 in.) wide with four or five pointed tepals. Thrives in gritty garden soils enriched with humus. Not suited for heavy, clay soils. Best planted in front of an herbaceous or mixed border and allowed to scramble over neighbouring plants. Zones 3–9.

Clematis 'Lord Nevill'

Hardy, moderately vigorous, deciduous climber 2.4–3 m (7.75–10 ft.) tall. Pruning group 2. Flowering from late spring to early summer and again in late summer. Striking, single, deep blue flowers, 15–20 cm (6–8 in.) across, are composed of six to eight veined, textured tepals with wavy margins. The tepals overlap at the base and smartly taper to fine points. Best in part shade to prevent premature fading of flower color. Shows up well against a light background. Suitable for growing on a trellis, obelisk, or pergola. May also be grown with other wall-trained shrubs which do not require annual pruning. Zones 4–9.

Clematis 'Louise Rowe'

A unique cultivar which bears pale lilac double, semi-double, and single flowers simultaneously. Hardy, not-too-vigorous, compact, deciduous climber 1.2–1.8 m (3.5–6 ft.) tall. Pruning group 2. Flowering from early to midsummer and again in early autumn. Semi-double and double flowers, 12.5–15 cm (5–6 in.) across, vary from pale mauve to almost greyish white depending on the light level and the flower's maturity. The rounded yet pointed tepals are arranged in rows, the secondary rows with scalloped margins. Some tepals are twisted, giving the flower a frilly appearance. Single flowers, borne on the current season's wood, are somewhat paler in color and are composed of six tepals. Ideal for container culture or for growing as a specimen plant on a small obelisk or trellis. Zones 4–9.

Clematis 'Lunar Lass'

Evergreen/Forsteri Group. Half-hardy, evergreen, non-clinging, trailing shrub 30–50 cm (12–20 in.) tall. Pruning group 1. Flowering from mid to late

Clematis 'Lord Nevill'. Photo by J. Lindmark.

Clematis 'Louise Rowe'. Photo by E. Leeds.

Clematis 'Lunar Lass'. Photo by E. Leeds.

spring. Single, pale green flowers consist of four or five, occasionally six, tepals, each 1–1.8 cm (0.5–0.75 in.) long. Seedheads are distinctly hairy. The small, dark green leaves are leathery and firm. Thrives in well-drained soil in a warm position. Best for container culture in a cold greenhouse or conservatory, or plunged in an alpine bed under glass. May be grown in a raised bed in warmer climes. Zones 8–9.

Clematis 'Luther Burbank'

Hardy, vigorous, strong-growing, deciduous climber 3–4 m (10–13 ft.) tall. Pruning group 3. Flowering from early to late summer. Large, single, violet-purple flowers, 13–20 cm (5–8 in.) in diameter, are composed of six rounded tepals with undulating margins. Reverse of tepals has a white downy surface. Shows up well against a light background. Grow naturally through a small tree or shrub, or with a moderately vigorous climbing rose. Suitable as a specimen plant on a medium-sized obelisk or free-standing trellis in a mixed border. May also be grown for a short term in a large container. Zones 4–9.

Clematis 'M. Koster'

Viticella Group. Synonym: *C. viticella* 'Margot Koster'. Hardy, moderately vigorous, compact, deciduous climber 2.5–3 m (8–10 ft.) tall. Pruning group 3. Flowering from summer to early autumn. Single, deep mauvish pink, semi-nodding flowers, up to 10 cm (4 in.) across, are borne freely and consist of four to six tepals, recurved at the margins and tips. With age the tepals literally roll back on themselves, giving the flowers a gappy, loose, untidy appearance. Best flower color in sun or part shade. Suitable for short-term container culture. Partner it with a climbing rose or large shrub. Zones 3–9.

Clematis macropetala

Atragene Group. An easy to grow, delightful and floriferous species. Hardy, moderately vigorous, deciduous climber or scrambler 2–3 m (6.5–10 ft.) tall. Native to northern China, eastern Mongolia, and eastern Siberia. Pruning group 1. Flowering in spring with occasional flowers in late summer. Numerous, single, pale blue to purple-blue flowers are made of four tepals, each 3–4.5

Clematis 'Luther Burbank'. Photo by M. Toomey.

Clematis 'M. Koster'. Photo by J. Lindmark.

Clematis macropetala. Photo by R. Evison.

Clematis 'Madame Baron-Veillard'. Photo by C. Chesshire.

cm (1.25–1.75 in.) long. The tepals enclose numerous petal-like staminodes (sterile stamens), ranging from the blue outer set to the inner cluster of bluish white, and giving the appearance of a double flower. Seedheads are numerous. Best in sharply draining garden soils enriched with humus. Suitable for any aspect, including cold and windy sites such as a north- or northeast-facing wall. Ideal for container culture. Grow on a pergola or through a small tree or medium-sized shrub which does not require annual pruning. Zones 3–9.

Clematis 'Madame Baron-Veillard'

A welcome, exceptionally late-flowering cultivar for the autumn garden. Hardy, vigorous, deciduous climber 3–4 m (10–13 ft.) tall. Pruning group 3. Flowering from early to midautumn. Single, dusky midmauvish pink flowers are 10–13 cm (4–5 in.) wide, with six to eight blunt, overlapping tepals, each with textured margins and with grooves running along the centre. With age, the tepals recurve slightly at their tips. Best in full sun. Ideal to grow naturally through medium-sized shrubs or trees or with other wall-trained climbers. Suitable for an arbour, pergola, or large trellis. Zones 4–9.

Clematis 'Madame Édouard André'

RHS Award of Garden Merit (1993). Hardy, not-too-vigorous, compact, deciduous climber 1.8–2.4 m (6–7.75 ft.) tall. Pruning group 3. Flowering from late spring to late summer. Single, wine-red flowers, 10–12.5 cm (4–5 in.) across, remain slightly cupped on opening and ultimately become flat. Flower color ages to a more mauvish red. The four to six, rounded but pointed tepals are slightly flecked with white and have incurving margins. Ideal for short-term container culture or for growing over prostrate conifers and other medium-sized shrubs. Suitable for a small to medium-sized obelisk or trellis. Zones 4–9.

Clematis 'Madame Édouard André'. Photo by C. Chesshire.

Clematis 'Madame Grangé'

RHS First Class Certificate (1877), RHS Award of Garden Merit (1993). Hardy, moderately vigorous, deciduous climber 2.4–3 m (7.75–10 ft.) tall. Pruning group 3. Flowering from mid to late summer. Single, rich, velvety, dusky purple flowers are 12.5–15 cm (5–6 in.) across and composed of four to six tepals, each with a concentration of red along the middle. The tepals have incurving margins and open out fully with age, rendering the flowers flat. Reverse of tepals distinguished by a silvery purple coloring. Best in sun or part shade. Shows up well against a light background or with plants which have light-colored foliage. Suitable for a medium-sized trellis or obelisk, or for training through small trees or large shrubs. Zones 4–9.

Clematis 'Madame Julia Correvon'

Viticella Group. RHS Award of Garden Merit (1993). Synonym: *C. viticella* 'Madame Julia Correvon'. Hardy, moderately vigorous, deciduous

Clematis 'Madame Grangé'. Photo by J. Lindmark.

climber 3–4 m (10–13 ft.) tall. Pruning group 3. Flowering from mid to late summer. Single, vibrant, rich claret red, semi-nodding flowers, 7–10 cm (2.25–4 in.) wide, unfold from slightly twisted buds and become gappy with age. Four to six narrow tepals are deeply veined down the midrib and have somewhat scalloped and recurving margins. Best in sun or part shade. Grow on an obelisk or medium-sized, free-standing trellis or rustic fence. Partner it with a climbing rose. Allow to climb into small trees, conifers, or medium-sized to large, open shrubs. Zones 3–9.

Clematis 'Madame Julia Correvon'. Photo by E. Leeds.

Clematis mandschurica

Herbaceous Group. Hardy, sprawling, reluctantly climbing perennial that eventually reaches 0.9–1.5 m (3–5 ft.) tall at most. Pruning group 3. Native to northern China, Korea, and Mongolia. Flowering from mid to late summer. Numerous, small, single, pure white, scented flowers, 2–3 cm (0.75–1.25 in.) across, are borne on terminal shoots and in leaf axils. The four or five tepals are narrow and pointed. Suitable in any aspect but produces strongest scent in full sun. Best to allow the plant to find its support from neighbouring low-growing plants in a mixed border. Zones 3–9.

Clematis 'Margaret Hunt'

Hardy, very vigorous, deciduous climber 3–3.6 m (10–11.5 ft.) tall. Pruning group 3. Flowering from late spring to late summer. Medium-sized, single, lavender-pink, star-shaped flowers are 10–15 cm (4–6 in.) across and composed of four to six tepals. The tepals have a bluish tint when first open that fades away as the flower matures. Grow through a large shrub or on a pergola, arbour, or large obelisk. Zones 4–9.

Clematis mandschurica. Photo by E. Leeds.

Clematis 'Marie Boisselot'

RHS Award of Garden Merit (1993). A delightful cultivar with a long flowering period. Hardy, vigorous, deciduous climber 2.4–3 m (7.75–10 ft.) tall. Pruning optional, group 2, or group 3. A hard pruning (group 3) delays flowering. Flowering from early summer to early autumn. Large, single, satiny white flowers are 15–20 cm (6–8

Clematis 'Margaret Hunt'. Photo by J. Lindmark.

Clematis 'Marie Boisselot'. Photo by M. Toomey.

in.) wide and open flat. The eight broad, rounded tepals are overlapping and deeply grooved along the middle. Grow it naturally through and over a low-growing or prostrate conifer or medium-sized shrub which does not require annual pruning. Zones 4–9.

Clematis 'Marjorie'

Montana Group. Synonym: *C. montana* 'Marjorie'. Hardy, vigorous, deciduous climber 8 m (26 ft.) tall or taller. Pruning group 1. Flowering from late spring to early summer. Semi-double, creamy pink flowers have salmony petal-like staminodes (sterile stamens). Early spring flowers sometimes open with a green tinge due to insufficient sunlight, but the right color is restored as the season progresses and more light becomes available.

Thrives in sharply drained soils. Suitable for any aspect but produces best flower color in a warm, sunny position. Grow through a medium-sized to large tree or conifer. Absolutely superb when grown as a specimen plant on a very large pergola or pagoda. Zones 7–9.

Clematis 'Markham's Pink'

Atragene Group. RHS Award of Merit (1935), RHS Award of Garden Merit (1993). Synonyms: *C. macropetala* 'Markham's Pink', *C. macropetala* var. *markhamii*. Hardy, moderately vigorous, deciduous climber 2–2.5 m (6.5–8 ft.) tall. Pruning group 1. Flowering from mid to late spring. Double, clear, deep pink, nodding or semi-nodding, bell-shaped flowers are composed of four basal tepals, each 5 cm (2 in.) long and spreading with

Clematis 'Marjorie'. Photo by E. Leeds.

Clematis 'Markham's Pink'. Photo by S. Marczyński.

Clematis marmoraria early flowers are green, fading to almost white. Photo by I. Holmåsen.

age. The tepals surround an inner skirt of narrower, pointed tepal-like structures that give the flower a spiky appearance. Thrives in sharply drained soil. Suitable for any aspect but produces best flower color in sun. Good for small gardens. May be allowed to roam into medium-sized shrubs or small trees. Zones 3–9.

Clematis marmoraria

Evergreen Group. RHS Award of Merit (1988), RHS Award of Garden Merit (1993). A splendid plant. Half-hardy, low-growing, mound-forming, non-clinging, dwarf, suckering, evergreen alpine which grows slowly to 8–10 cm (3.25–4 in.) tall. Native to New Zealand. Pruning group 1. Flowering in early spring. Small, single, creamy white flowers, 2 cm (0.75 in.) across, are carried just above the foliage. The five, sometimes six to eight, broad tepals do not overlap and are rounded yet pointed. Flower buds are distinctly greenish. Best grown in a container in a cool greenhouse or conservatory. Also suitable for an alpine house or border. Protect from winter wet. Zones 8–9.

Clematis 'Matka Teresa'

Trade name: Mother Teresa. Hardy, moderately vigorous, compact, deciduous climber 1.8–2.4 m (6–7.75 ft.) tall. Pruning group 2. Flowering from late spring to late summer. Large, single, white flowers are 15–20 cm (6–8 in.) across and carry six to eight tepals with wavy margins. Tepals of young flowers carry a very pale mauve bar, which fades away with age. Best in sun or part shade. Requires a sheltered position to prevent wind damage to the flowers. Suitable for a small obelisk or trellis. May be grown in a large container for a short period. Zones 4–9.

Clematis 'Maureen'

RHS Award of Merit (1956). Hardy, not-too-vigorous, compact, deciduous climber 1.8–2.4 m (6–7.75 ft.) tall. Pruning group 3. Flowering from early summer to early autumn. Single, velvety purple-red flowers, 12–15 cm (4.75–6 in.) wide,

lose their lustre with age. The six broad, overlapping, slightly recurved tepals have gently undulating margins. Each tepal has a dash of red along the middle. Shows up well against a light background. Suitable for a small trellis or obelisk, or for growing through medium-sized shrubs. Ideal for short-term container culture or for cascading over a low wall. Zones 4–9.

Clematis 'Matka Teresa' (Mother Teresa). Photo by R. Savill.

Clematis 'Maureen'. Photo by C. Chesshire.

Clematis 'Mayleen'. Photo by C. Chesshire.

Clematis 'Mikelite'. Photo by E. Leeds.

Clematis 'Mayleen'

Montana Group. RHS Award of Garden Merit (2002). Synonym: *C. montana* 'Mayleen'. Hardy, vigorous, deciduous climber 6–8 m (20–26 ft.) tall or taller. Pruning group 1. Flowering from late spring to early summer. Single, deep pink, vanilla-scented, saucer-shaped flowers are 7.5 cm (3 in.) wide and composed of four somewhat rounded tepals. Thrives in sharply drained soils. Suitable for part shade but produces the best flower color and strongest scent in a sunny position. Grow through a medium-sized to large tree or conifer. Zones 7–9.

Clematis 'Mikelite'

Hardy, moderately vigorous, compact, deciduous climber 1.8–2.4 m (6–7.75 ft.) tall. Pruning group 3. Flowering from mid to late summer. Single, rich reddish purple flowers are 11–14 cm (4.5–5.5 in.) across with four to six broad yet pointed tepals which do not overlap. Each tepal has a slight rosy red bar along the centre. This bar is widest at the base and tapers towards the tip. Best in garden soils enriched with humus. Suitable for short-term container culture, or for a medium-sized obelisk or trellis. May be grown with another moderately vigorous clematis in pruning group 2. Zones 3–9.

Clematis 'Miniseelik'

Hardy, compact, deciduous climber 1.5–1.8 m (5–6 ft.) tall. Pruning group 3. Flowering from mid to late summer. Small, single, deep reddish purple flowers, 6–7 cm (2.25–2.75 in.) across, fade to purplish red with age. Each of the six tepals boasts a central white stripe, which takes on a pronounced red veining with age. Ideal for container culture or for growing over a low wall. May also be trained through a low shrub or prostrate conifer. Zones 4–9.

Clematis 'Minister'

Hardy, compact, deciduous climber 1.5–1.8 m (5–6 ft.) tall. Pruning group 2. Flowering from late spring to early summer and again in late summer. Single, lavender-blue flowers with a shading of purple are 18–20 cm (7–8 in.) across and are produced in abundance. They are composed of four to six

Clematis 'Miniseelik'. Photo by M. Toomey.

Clematis 'Minister'. Photo by E. Leeds.

Clematis 'Minuet'. Photo by J. Lindmark.

Clematis 'Miss Bateman'. Photo by J. Lindmark.

tepals. May be grown in a container or over a small shrub. Suitable for a small obelisk. Zones 4–9.

Clematis 'Minuet'

Viticella Group. RHS Award of Garden Merit (1993). Synonym: *C. viticella* 'Minuet'.

Hardy, moderately vigorous, compact, deciduous climber 2.5–3 m (8–10 ft.) tall. Pruning group 3. Flowering from midsummer to midautumn. Handsome, single, pale white, semi-nodding flowers are 6 cm (2.25 in.) across. The four tepals are blunt-tipped with pale purplish red deeply veined margins. Train it up a trellis or an obelisk. Grow through a medium-sized shrub. Zones 3–9.

Clematis 'Miss Bateman'

RHS First Class Certificate (1869), RHS Award of Garden Merit (1993). Hardy, moderately vigorous, compact, deciduous climber 1.8–2.4 m (6–7.75 ft.) tall. Pruning group 2. Flowering from late spring to early summer. Single, satiny white, rounded flowers, 14–15 cm (5.5–6 in.) across, are freely produced and consist of six to eight

Clematis montana var. *montana*. Photo by J. Lindmark.

translucent, overlapping, tapering tepals with blunt tips. A central green stripe distinctly displayed on the reverse of each tepal is characteristic of early flowers and those grown in the shade. Team it with other wall-trained or freestanding shrubs and roses which do not require annual pruning. Suitable for a small obelisk or trellis. Zones 4–9.

Clematis montana var. *montana*

Montana Group. Synonym: *C. montana* 'Alba'. Half-hardy, vigorous, deciduous climber to 8 m (26 ft.) tall or taller. Native to Himalaya and central and western China. Pruning group 1. Flowering from late spring to early summer. Single, white, somewhat flat flowers are borne in groups of one to five from the leaf axils of the previous season's ripened wood. There are four, rarely five, tepals, each 3–4 cm (1.25–1.5 in.) long. Best in sharply drained soils. Grow through tall trees and conifers, along a spacious boundary wall or sturdy fence, or over a pergola. May be grown as a ground cover. Zones 7–9.

Clematis montana var. *grandiflora*. Photo by J. Lindmark.

Clematis montana var. *grandiflora*

Montana Group. RHS Award of Garden Merit (1993). Synonym: *C. montana* 'Grandiflora'. Hardy, vigorous, deciduous climber to 12 m (39 ft.) tall or taller. Native to northern India. Pruning group 1. Flowering from mid to late spring. Single, pure white, saucer-shaped flowers are 10 cm

Clematis montana var. *rubens* 'Tetrarose'. Photo by R. Surman.

(4 in.) wide and are composed of four broad tepals with round edges. Best in well-drained garden soils. A perfect plant for a large garden. Grow through large trees and conifers. Suitable for a large pergola, wall, or boundary fence. Zones 6–9.

Clematis montana var. *rubens* 'Tetrarose'

Montana Group. RHS Award of Garden Merit (1993). Synonym: *C. montana* 'Tetrarose'. Half-hardy, vigorous, deciduous climber to 8 m (26 ft.) tall. Pruning group 1. Flowering from late spring to early summer. Large, single, satiny, deep mauve pink, spicy-scented flowers are 7.5 cm (3 in.) across and formed of four thick tepals which are slightly cup-shaped even when mature. Stems are reddish brown and leaves are bronzy green. Best in sun or part shade. Keep clear of frost pockets. Grow through a medium-sized to large tree or conifer. Looks well along a boundary wall or fence, or over a pergola. Zones 7–9.

Clematis 'Monte Cassino'

Hardy, vigorous, strong-growing, deciduous climber 2.4–3 m (7.75–10 ft.) tall. Pruning optional, group 2, or group 3. A hard pruning (group 3) results in the loss of early flowers. Flowering from late spring to early summer and again in late summer. Single, velvety reddish purple, well-rounded flowers are 15–20 cm (6–8 in.) across. Six wide, overlapping tepals have irregularly notched edges. Best in good light but not strong sunlight. Shows up well against a light background. Allow to grow through medium-sized shrubs. Suitable for a medium-sized obelisk, arch, or pergola. May be grown in a very large container for a short period. Zones 4–9.

Clematis 'Moonlight'

Hardy, weak-growing, deciduous climber 2.4–3 m (7.75–10 ft.) tall. Pruning group 2. Flowering from late spring to early summer and again in late summer. Single, pale cream-yellow flowers are 15–20 cm (6–8 in.) wide with six to eight over-

Clematis 'Monte Cassino'.
Photo by S. Marczyński.

Clematis 'Moonlight'.
Photo by Y. Aihara.

Clematis 'Mrs Cholmondeley'. Photo by R. Surman.

lapping tepals. The tepals tend to twist with age and occasionally show a dash of green. Best in part shade to prevent premature fading of flower color. Requires a sheltered position to prevent wind damage to the flowers. Shows up well against a dark background. Grow on a trellis, pergola, or arch. May be carefully trained through moderately vigorous shrubs which do not require annual pruning. Zones 4–9.

Clematis 'Mrs Cholmondeley'

RHS First Class Certificate (1873), RHS Award of Garden Merit (1993). Hardy, vigorous, deciduous climber 3–3.6 m (10–11.5 ft.) tall. Pruning optional, group 2, or group 3. A hard pruning (group 3) results in the loss of early flowers. Flowering from late spring to late summer. Very large, single, light blue-mauve, gappy flowers are 15–20 cm (6–8 in.) across and are composed of six to eight tepals which do not overlap. Each tepal tapers towards its base and is deeply veined along the midrib, which is also slightly paler in color. Requires a sheltered position to prevent wind damage to the flowers. Grow on a large trellis, obelisk, pergola, or arch. May be trained through a robust large shrub which does not require annual pruning. Zones 4–9.

Clematis 'Mrs George Jackman'

RHS First Class Certificate (1875), RHS Award of Garden Merit (1993). A very old cultivar. Hardy, moderately vigorous, deciduous climber 1.8–2.4 m (6–7.75 ft.) tall. Pruning group 2. Flowering from late spring to early summer and again from late summer to early autumn. Semi-double, satiny, creamy white flowers of the first flush, produced on old wood from the previous season, are 15–18 cm (6–7 in.) across with six to eight broad, pointed, overlapping basal tepals. Further layers of short tepals surmount those at the base. A second flush of flowers, these single, is produced on the current season's new growth. Grow on a small to medium-sized obelisk or trellis. Suitable for short-term container culture. Zones 4–9.

Clematis 'Mrs George Jackman'. Photo by M. Toomey.

Clematis 'Mrs James Mason' (single flower). Photo by E. Leeds.

Clematis 'Mrs James Mason'

Hardy, moderately vigorous, compact, deciduous climber 1.8–2.4 m (6–7.75 ft.) tall. Pruning group 2. Flowering from late spring to early summer and again from late summer to early autumn. Large, semi-double, violet-blue flowers of the first flush, borne on old wood from the previous season, are 15–18 cm (6–7 in.) across with eight broad, boat-shaped, somewhat overlapping basal tepals. Each tepal has a velvety dark red bar along the centre and undulating frilly margins. Several shorter inner rows of lilac-blue tepals tower above the basal row of vibrantly colored tepals, almost eclipsing them. Flowers of the second flush, borne profusely on the current season's new growth, are single. Requires a sheltered position to prevent wind damage to the flowers. Grow on a small to medium-sized pergola or trellis. Zones 4–9.

Clematis 'Mrs N. Thompson'

Hardy, weak-growing, compact, deciduous climber 1.8–2.4 m (6–7.75 ft.) tall. Pruning group 2. Flowering from late spring to early summer and again in early autumn. Striking, single, rich purple-blue flowers are 12.5–15 cm (5–6 in.) wide and made of six to eight broad yet tapering tepals, each boasting a vivid scarlet central bar and slightly scalloped margins. Reverse side of each tepal has a greenish cream bar fading to pinkish purple at the margins. Best in full sun or part shade. Can be slow to establish itself. Suitable for short-term container culture. Grow on a small to medium-sized obelisk or trellis. Zones 4–9.

Clematis 'Mrs P. B. Truax'

Hardy, moderately vigorous, compact, deciduous climber 1.8–2.4 m (6–7.75 ft.) tall. Pruning group 2. Flowering from late spring to early summer and again in early autumn. Medium-sized, single, periwinkle blue flowers, 12.5–15 cm (5–6 in.) across, fade to light blue with age and are made of six to eight rounded but pointed tepals. Best in sun or part shade. Grow in a container or as a specimen plant on a medium-sized obelisk or

Clematis 'Mrs N. Thompson'. Photo by C. Chesshire.

Clematis 'Mrs P. B. Truax'. Photo by C. Chesshire.

Clematis 'Mrs P. T. James'. Photo by J. Lindmark.

Clematis 'Mrs Robert Brydon' growing through a picket fence with buddleia. Photo by C. Chesshire.

trellis. May be teamed with a moderately vigorous shrub which does not require annual pruning. Zones 4–9.

Clematis 'Mrs P. T. James'

Hardy, not-too-vigorous, compact, deciduous climber 1.8–2.4 m (6–7.75 ft.) tall. Pruning group 2. Flowering from early to late summer. Single, violet-blue, open flowers are 12–18 cm (4.75–7 in.) across. Each of the six to eight broad yet pointed, overlapping tepals has a silvery blue sheen along the centre and prominent veining and texturing. Best in garden soils enriched with humus. Grow on a small to medium-sized obelisk or trellis, or as a companion for a wall-trained shrub not requiring a heavy, annual pruning. Zones 4–9.

Clematis 'Mrs Robert Brydon'

Herbaceous/Heracleifolia Group. Hardy, deciduous, non-clinging, herbaceous perennial 1.8–2.4 m (6–7.75 ft.) tall. Pruning group 3. Flowering from midsummer to early autumn. Single, bluish white flowers are 3 cm (1.25 in.) wide and carry four or five narrow tepals which roll back on themselves. Best in moist, free-draining soils. If trained on an artificial support, the stems will need tying-in. Good for covering old tree stumps or as a ground cover. Zones 4–9.

Clematis 'Mrs T. Lundell'

Viticella Group. Synonyms: *C.* 'Mrs Tage Lundell', *C. viticella* 'Mrs T. Lundell'. Hardy, moderately vigorous, deciduous climber 2.5–3 m (8–10 ft.) tall. Pruning group 3. Flowering from midsummer to

Clematis 'Mrs T. Lundell'. Photo by J. Lindmark.

early autumn. Single, pale bluish violet flowers, 7.5–9 cm (3–3.5 in.) across, are semi-nodding at first, opening flat, and becoming cross-shaped with age. The four blunt tepals are slightly recurving. May be allowed to climb into small to medium-sized trees or open shrubs. Suitable on a low trellis or obelisk. Zones 3–9.

Clematis 'Multi Blue'

Hardy, moderately vigorous, deciduous climber 1.8–2.4 m (6–7.75 ft.) tall. Pruning group 2. Flowering from late spring to early summer and again from late summer to early autumn. Fully double, rich navy blue, well-rounded flowers, 10–12.5 cm (4–5 in.) wide, are borne on old wood of the previous season. These are formed of six to eight basal tepals topped with many inner layers of shorter, narrower, and more pointed reddish purple–blue tepals with white tips. The arrangement confers a spiky appearance on the central crown of the flower. Each tepal boasts a light green central bar on the re-

verse. Inner tepals remain after the outer tepals wither and fall away. Flowers of the second flush, borne on new growth of the current season, are semi-double but otherwise similar in shape and form to the early double flowers. Best in sun or part shade. Requires a sheltered position to prevent wind damage to the flowers. Grow on a small obelisk or trellis. Ideal for short-term container culture. Zones 4–9.

Clematis napaulensis

Evergreen Group. RHS Award of Merit (1957). Synonym: *C. forrestii*. Half-hardy, vigorous, semi-evergreen climber to 7.7 m (25 ft.) tall. Native to Himalaya, southern Tibet, and southwestern China. Pruning group 1. Flowering from winter to early spring. Unusual, small, single, creamy yellow to greenish white, nodding, bell-shaped, solitary flowers, 1.6–1.8 cm (0.5–0.75 in.) across, are borne in short-stemmed clusters of up to 10 in a pair of leaf nodes. Each flower is carried on a hairy stalk with a pair of fused, hairy, greenish,

Clematis 'Multi Blue'. Photo by E. Leeds.

Clematis napaulensis. Photo by E. Leeds.

Clematis 'Natacha'. Photo by R. Savill.

Clematis 'Negritianka'. Photo by J. Lindmark.

cupped, leaf-like growths (bracts) midway along the stalk. There are four tepals, each 1.5–2.5 cm (0.5–1 in.) long, rolled back or recurved at the tip. Stamens consist of prominent purple filaments and anthers which protrude from the flower by almost the length of the tepals. Young shoots are greyish, and the grooved stems become woody with age. Leaves are bright green and congested. During its period of dormancy in midsummer, the plant may lose its leaves. Best in well-drained soils. Requires a warm, sheltered position, such as a south-facing wall. Can look drab in summer, so choose the planting position carefully. Makes a good conservatory or cool greenhouse plant. Zones 7–9.

Clematis 'Natacha'

Hardy, moderately vigorous, compact, deciduous climber 1.8–2.4 m (6–7.75 ft.) tall. Pruning group 2. Flowering from late spring to early summer and again in late summer. Single, lavender-violet

Clematis 'Nelly Moser'. Photo by M. Toomey.

flowers, 10–14 cm (4–5.5 in.) across, carry six to eight broad, oval, overlapping tepals with gently undulating margins. As the flower matures, the central bar running from the base to the tip in each tepal takes on a lighter shade. Best in garden soils enriched with humus. Suitable for a medium-sized obelisk or trellis. Partner it with a low-growing shrub which does not require annual pruning. Zones 3–9.

Clematis 'Negritianka'

Hardy, moderately vigorous, deciduous climber 2.4–3 m (7.75–10 ft.) tall. Pruning group 3. Flowering from mid to late summer. A profusion of single, rich plum purple flowers, 10–13 cm (4–5 in.) wide, with five or six well-formed, rounded tepals. Shows up well against a light background. Grow through a medium-sized shrub or small tree, preferably with silver or golden leaves. Ideal for a trellis, obelisk, or pergola. Zones 4–9.

Clematis 'Nelly Moser'

RHS Award of Garden Merit (1993). An excellent, very old cultivar. Hardy, vigorous, deciduous climber 2.4–3 m (7.75–10 ft.) tall or taller. Floriferous when established. Pruning group 2. Flowering from late spring to early summer and again in early autumn. Single, pale mauvish pink flowers,

15–20 cm (6–8 in.) wide, consist of six to eight pointed, overlapping tepals, each with a distinct deeper pink central bar. White filaments carrying dark red anthers bring vibrancy to the well-held, fully open, flattish flowers. Large, globular seed-heads. Best in part or full shade, preferably a north-facing aspect, to prevent fading of flower color. Partner it with a large shrub or small tree which does not require annual pruning. May be trained up a medium-sized obelisk, arch, or trellis. Zones 4–9.

Clematis 'New Love'

Herbaceous/Heracleifolia Group. Synonym: *C. heracleifolia* 'New Love'. Hardy, non-clinging, woody-based, deciduous, compact, rounded subshrub 0.6–0.8 m (2–2.75 ft.) tall. Pruning group 3. Flowering from midsummer to early autumn. Single, pale violet-blue, tubular, hyacinth-like, fragrant flowers, 2–2.5 cm (0.75–1 in.) long, are held above the foliage and carry four tepals with spreading and recurving tips. Outside of the flower is a darker shade of violet blue. Best in moist, well-drained garden soils. Suitable for sun or shade. Plant at the front of mixed or herbaceous borders. Grows well in a large container. Zones 5–9.

Clematis 'Nikolai Rubtsov'

Synonym: *C.* 'Nikolaj Rubtzov'. Hardy, moderately vigorous, deciduous climber 2.4–3 m (7.75–10 ft.) tall. Pruning group 3. Flowering from mid to late summer. Single, reddish lilac flowers, 10–14 cm (4–5.5 in.) across, are borne profusely or sometimes moderately. Each of the four to six tepals has a paler lilac central bar. Suitable for a medium-sized obelisk or trellis. Grow with a small to medium-sized shrub or tree. Zones 4–9.

Clematis 'New Love'. Photo by C. Chesshire.

Clematis 'Nikolai Rubtsov'. Photo by C. Chesshire.

Clematis 'Odoriba'. Photo courtesy Ozawa Slide Library.

Clematis 'Niobe'

RHS Award of Garden Merit (1993). A superb, universally popular cultivar. Hardy, not-too-vigorous, deciduous climber 1.8–2.4 m (6–7.75 ft.) tall. Pruning group 2 or 3. A hard pruning (group 3) results in the loss of early flowers. Flowering from late spring to early autumn.

Single, velvety ruby red flowers, 12.5–15 cm (5–6 in.) wide, open wide and fade to a deep wine-red with age. The six to eight tepals are broad at the base and tapering towards the tips. Best flower color in sun, although color will fade quickly. Suitable as a specimen plant in the garden or in a container. Team it with a moderately vigorous climbing rose. Zones 4–9.

Clematis 'Odoriba'

An excellent, long-flowering Japanese cultivar with small flowers. Hardy, moderately vigorous, deciduous climber 2.5–3 m (8–10 ft.) tall or taller. Pruning group 3. Flowering from early summer to autumn. An abundance of single, slightly nodding, dark pink flowers, 2.5–3.5 cm (1–1.6 in.) across, are borne on new growth of the current season. The four tepals, which spread with age, are white at the base and have recurved tips. Best in well-drained, fertile soil and away from full sun. Train it up an obelisk or trellis or team it with a dark-flowered clematis such as 'Star of India'. Zones 6–9.

Clematis 'Niobe'. Photo by S. Marczyński.

Clematis 'Olimpiada-80'

Hardy, moderately vigorous, deciduous climber 2.4–3 m (7.75–10 ft.) tall. Attractive flowers. Pruning group 2. Flowering during late spring and again from mid to late summer. Single, bright crimson red, gappy flowers are 16–18 cm (6.25–7 in.) across with four to six pointed tepals. Each tepal has a brighter colored central bar. Suitable for a medium-sized trellis, obelisk, arbour, or pergola. Grow with a moderately vigorous shrub which does not require annual pruning. Zones 4–9.

Clematis 'Pagoda'

Viticella Group. RHS Award of Garden Merit (2002). Synonyms: *C. viticella* 'Pagoda', *C. texensis* 'Pagoda'. Hardy, not-too-vigorous, neat-growing and compact, deciduous climber 1.8–2.5 m (6–7.75 ft.) tall. Pruning group 3. Prune back the

flowered stems of midsummer to encourage a second flush of flowers and also to keep the plant tidy. Flowering from early summer to early autumn. Single, pale white, gently nodding, bell-shaped flowers are 4–5 cm (1.5–2 in.) long and made up of four tepals with mauvish pink margins and distinct veining. Reverse of each tepal has a prominent purple-pink central bar. The tepals recurve generously, curling and twisting at the tips with age. May be prone to mildew. Good for a short obelisk or team it with a moderately vigorous climbing rose. Zones 3–9.

Clematis 'Pamela Jackman'

Atragene Group. Synonym: *C. alpina* 'Pamela Jackman'. Hardy, not-too-vigorous, deciduous climber 2–3 m (6.5–10 ft.) tall or taller. Pruning group 1. Flowering from mid to late spring with occasional flowers in late summer. Small, single,

Clematis 'Olimpiada-80'. Photo by M. A. Beskaravainaja.

Clematis 'Pagoda'. Photo by C. Chesshire.

Clematis 'Pamela Jackman'. Photo by C. Chesshire.

deep blue, nodding flowers have four, short, pointed tepals, each 4 cm (1.5 in.) long. The tepals surround a central tuft of staminodes composed of pale bluish outer staminodes and creamy colored inner staminodes. Best in free-draining garden soils. Grow with other wall-trained shrubs which require little or no annual pruning. Train it up a free-standing trellis, obelisk, or similar artificial support. Ideal for container culture. Zones 3–9.

Clematis
'Pamiat Serdtsa'.
Photo by J. Lindmark.

Clematis
'Pangbourne Pink'.
Photo by J. Lindmark.

Clematis 'Pamiat Serdtsa'

Herbaceous Group. Synonyms: *C.* 'Pamjat Serdtsa', *C.* 'Pamjatj Serdtza', *C.* 'Pamjatj Sertsa'. Hardy, semi-herbaceous, normally non-clinging, compact semi-shrub 1.5–2 m (5–6.5 ft.) tall. Pruning group 3. Flowering from mid to late summer. Single, satiny, pale lilac-mauve, nodding, broadly bell-shaped, delicate flowers, 5–8 cm (2–3.25 in.) wide, are borne in groups of one to three on new shoots of the current year. The four to six wide tepals twist and are slightly recurving. Young stems are hairy and brownish or reddish. If trained on an artificial support, the stems need tying-in. Allow to scramble through a medium-sized shrub in a mixed border or plant in herbaceous borders and provide support. Zones 3–9.

Clematis 'Pangbourne Pink'

Herbaceous/Integrifolia Group. RHS Award of Garden Merit (2002). Synonym: *C. integrifolia* 'Pangbourne Pink'. Hardy, deciduous, non-clinging, woody-based herbaceous perennial or subshrub 0.6 m (2 ft.) tall. Pruning group 3. Flowering from early summer to autumn. Single, deep pinkish mauve, open, bell-shaped, nodding flowers

are 5 cm (2 in.) wide and carry four tepals. The tepals have a brighter color with slight ribbing inside and a more smoky shade with deep ribbing on the outside. Tepal margins of the top half tend to recurve. Best in well-drained but moisture-retentive soil. May require some support such as unobtrusive pea-sticks. Grow at the front of an herbaceous or mixed border. Zones 3–9.

Clematis paniculata

Evergreen Group. Half-hardy, moderately vigorous, evergreen climber 3–4.5 m (10–14.5 ft.) tall. Native to New Zealand. Pruning group 1. Flowering from early to late spring. Single, pure white, semi-nodding, starry, fragrant flowers are 5 cm (2 in.) across with six to eight tepals. Male and female flowers are borne profusely on separate plants, the male flowers slightly larger than the female. Female plants produce abundant silvery, fluffy seedheads in autumn. Leaves are made of three dark green, somewhat leathery, shiny leaflets, each with a brownish central bar. Thrives in sharply drained soil and a warm position in front of a south-facing wall or other support in frost-free gardens. Slow to establish itself in the

Clematis paniculata. Photo by M. Toomey.

Clematis 'Pastel Blue'. Photo by C. Chesshire.

Clematis 'Pastel Pink'. Photo by C. Chesshire.

open garden. Best grown in a cool greenhouse or conservatory where the exquisite flowers can be enjoyed without damage from the weather. An excellent plant for a sheltered maritime garden. Zones 7–9.

Clematis 'Pastel Blue'

Herbaceous/Integrifolia Group. Synonym: *C. integrifolia* 'Pastel Blue'. Hardy, deciduous, non-clinging, herbaceous perennial 0.6 m (2 ft.) tall. Has a long flowering period. Pruning group 3. Flowering from early spring to late summer. Single, light blue, bell-shaped, slightly scented flowers are borne in clusters of up to 12 on a stem. The four pointed tepals, each 5–6 cm (2–2.25 in.) long, have crimped margins. Best in garden soils enriched with humus. Suitable for any aspect but produces strongest scent in a sunny position. May require some support. Ideal for the front half of an herbaceous or mixed border. Zones 3–9.

Clematis 'Pastel Pink'

Herbaceous/Integrifolia Group. Synonym: *C. integrifolia* 'Pastel Pink'. Hardy, deciduous, non-clinging, herbaceous perennial 0.6 m (2 ft.) tall. Pruning group 3. Flowering from early to late summer. Single, pale pink, nodding, bell-shaped, scented flowers are borne in clusters and carry four tepals. Each tepal is 4.5–5 cm (1.75–2 in.) long and has slightly scalloped margins. Best in garden soils enriched with humus. Grows in any aspect but produces strongest scent in a sunny position. May need some support. Suitable for the front of an herbaceous border. Zones 3–9.

Clematis 'Paul Farges'

RHS Award of Garden Merit (2002). Trade name: Summer Snow. Synonym: *C.* 'Fargesioides'. Hardy, vigorous, deciduous climber 4.6–6 m (15–20 ft.) tall or slightly more. Pruning group 3. Flowering from midsummer to early autumn. An abundance of single, creamy white, gappy, open flowers, 4–5 cm (1.5–2 in.) across, are held above the main stems on long stalks in clusters from the leaf axils. Some clones are scented. The four to six tepals are arrow-shaped and blunt-tipped. Mature stems are ridged and purplish brown. Useful

Clematis 'Paul Farges' (Summer Snow). Photo by J. Lindmark.

Clematis 'Perle d'Azur'. Photo by E. Leeds.

Clematis 'Perrin's Pride'. Photo by R. Savill.

for covering large areas of a fence or wall. May be trained over a pergola. Grow through medium-sized to large, open trees and conifers with dark foliage. Attractive when grown as a ground cover, space permitting. Best in a spacious garden. Zones 3–9.

Clematis 'Perle d'Azur'

RHS Award of Garden Merit (1993). Hardy, vigorous, deciduous climber 3–3.6 m (10–11.5 ft.) tall. A first-class, extremely floriferous plant which deserves to be widely grown. Pruning group 3. Flowering from mid to late summer. Single, translucent midblue, slightly nodding, somewhat rounded flowers, 10–12.5 cm (4–5 in.) across, fade slightly with age to a pinky azure blue. The four to six broad tepals, boasting a hint of pink on the central bars, recurve gently along the edges and at the tips. Lower parts of the vines tend to become naked as they lose the old, withered, and brown leaves. Very vibrant in sun but suitable for any aspect. Takes time to establish itself and is susceptible to wilt as a young plant. Prone to mildew. Useful for a pergola, arbour, or large obelisk. Team it with large shrubs, medium-sized trees, or conifers. Associates splendidly with climbing roses. Zones 4–9.

Clematis 'Perrin's Pride'

Hardy, moderately vigorous, deciduous climber 2.4–3 m (7.75–10 ft.) tall. Flowers on old and new wood, more abundantly on the new shoots. Pruning group 3. If early large flowers are required, leave a few old vines unpruned. Flowering from early to late summer. Single, soft purple, well-formed, somewhat rounded flowers, 10–15 cm (4–6 in.) wide, carry four to six overlapping, gently recurved tepals, each with a slightly darker shaded central bar. Grow naturally up and over large shrubs and medium-sized trees, or on a trellis, pergola, or arch. Zones 4–9.

Clematis 'Phoenix'

A floriferous plant with impressive, well-held large flowers. Hardy, strong-growing, deciduous climber 2–2.5 m (6.5–8 ft.) tall. Pruning group 2.

Flowering from late spring to early summer and again from mid summer to early autumn. Single, blue-violet flowers, 15–25 cm (6–10 in.) across, turn deep mauve and consist of six to eight overlapping tepals, each with a petunia-red bar and wrinkled and wavy margins. Flowers of first flush are larger than those of the second flush. Best in a sunny position. Grow as a specimen plant on a pillar, trellis, or obelisk. Zones 4–9.

Clematis 'Piilu'

Hardy, not-too-vigorous, very compact, deciduous climber 1.2–1.5 m (3.5–5 ft.) tall. Pruning group 1 or 2. Flowering from late spring to early

Clematis 'Phoenix'. Photo by M. Toomey.

Clematis 'Piilu'. Photo by M. Toomey.

summer and again in late summer. Flowers of the first flush are double. Flowers of the second flush are single, pale mauvish pink becoming paler towards the margins, upright, open, spreading, and 9–11 cm (3.5–4.5 in.) across. Each of the four to six overlapping, oval tepals has a deeper pink central bar and scalloped margins. Numerous tepal-like structures, which are modified spoon-shaped sterile stamens, confer the double appearance on the handsome flowers. Seedheads are an attractive golden brown. Best in full

Clematis 'Piilu', flower detail. Photo by M. Toomey.

sun. Suitable for container culture. Train on a small trellis or obelisk. May be partnered with a medium-sized, moderately vigorous shrub which does not require pruning. Zones 4–9.

Clematis 'Pink Fantasy'

Hardy, moderately vigorous, compact, deciduous climber 1.8–2.4 m (6–7.75 ft.) tall. Has a long flowering period. Pruning group 2 or 3. A hard pruning (group 3) results in the loss of early flowers. Flowering from summer to autumn. Single, shell-pink flowers, 11.5–14 cm (4.5–5.5 in.) wide, carry six to eight pointed tepals, each with scalloped margins and a deeper pink central bar which is more prominent toward its base. Tepals are inclined to twist, giving rise to an irregularly shaped flower. As the tepals age, their color fades to pale pink or even whitish pink. Best in part shade to prevent premature fading of flower color. A superb plant for containers or raised beds. May be grown horizontally by pegging down the vines to hold them in place and show off the blooms. Grow on a small trellis or obelisk or over a low shrub which does not require severe pruning. Zones 4–9.

Clematis 'Pink Fantasy'. Photo by M. Toomey.

Clematis 'Pink Flamingo'. Photo by J. Lindmark.

Clematis 'Pink Flamingo'

Atragene Group. RHS Award of Garden Merit (2002). Synonym: *C. alpina* 'Pink Flamingo'. Hardy, moderately vigorous, deciduous climber 2.5–3 m (8–10 ft.) tall. Pruning group 1. Flowering from mid to late spring, with occasional flowers in late summer. Semi-double, pale pink, semi-nodding flowers are 4 cm (1.5 in.) long and composed of tepals with deeper pink veining. Best in well-drained soils. Suitable for any aspect, especially north- or east-facing ones. Ideal for a small garden or container culture. Zones 3–9.

Clematis 'Pink Pearl'

Hardy, not-too-vigorous, compact, deciduous climber 1.8–2.4 m (6–7.75 ft.) tall. Pruning group 2. Flowering from mid to late spring and again in late summer. Single, pearly pink flowers, 10–15 cm (4–6 in.) across, carry six to eight broad, rounded, overlapping tepals with mauvish pink central veining. Best in garden soils enriched with humus. Good for container culture or for a medium-sized trellis or obelisk. Zones 4–9.

Clematis 'Pixie'

Evergreen Group. Hardy, evergreen, trailing shrub 46–61 cm (18–24 in.) tall. Pruning group 1. Flowering from early to midspring in the garden, often earlier under glass. Single, pale yellow-green flowers, 30–35 mm (ca. 1.25 in.) across, are borne in small clusters of five or more from the leaf axils. The flowers are bell-shaped at first, opening flat as they mature. Tepals number five, six, or eight and are oval to somewhat longer than broad with rounded tips. Each tepal is smooth above and hairy beneath. Only male flowers are produced. Leaves are much-divided, thick, and firm. Thrives in sharp-draining, gritty compost. Best in sun or part shade. Shelter from frost. For best results grow in a cold greenhouse or conservatory, or in a raised bed in the garden. Zones 7–9.

Clematis 'Polish Spirit'

RHS Award of Garden Merit (1993). Hardy, strong-growing, deciduous climber 2.5–3 m (8–10 ft.) tall. Pruning group 3. Flowering from midsummer to early autumn. Single, dark velvety purple, open flowers, 5–10 cm (2.5–4 in.)

Clematis 'Pink Pearl'.
Photo by J. Lindmark.

Clematis 'Pixie'. Photo
by E. Leeds.

Clematis 'Polish Spirit',
flower detail. Photo
by E. Leeds.

Clematis 'Polish Spirit'. Photo by S. Marczyński.

wide, are produced in abundance. The four to six tepals, each up to 9 cm (3.5 in.) across and with a light bar along the midrib, have blunt tips. Team it with a suitable climbing rose or grow through a medium-sized shrub with silver or gold foliage. May be trained against a pillar. Shows up well against a light background. Zones 3–9.

Clematis potaninii. Photo by J. Lindmark.

Clematis potaninii

Vitalba Group. Synonym: *C. fargesii* var. *souliei*. Hardy, vigorous, deciduous climber 3–5 m (10–16 ft.) tall. Native to western and southwestern China. Pruning group 3. Flowering from early summer to early autumn. Single, white or creamy white, flattish flowers, 4.5–7 cm (1.75–2.75 in.) across, are borne laterally and number from one to three in a small flowerhead. The five to seven broad, rounded, widely spreading tepals with gently undulating margins have three to five longitudinal veins. The very strongly ribbed stems are green, sometimes shaded with purple or violet. Best in well-drained soils. Very effective with medium-sized conifers, evergreen shrubs, or late-flowering, deep-colored roses. Suitable for a large pergola or trellis. Zones 3–9.

Clematis 'Poulala'

RHS Award of Garden Merit (2002). Trade name: Alabast. Hardy, moderately vigorous, deciduous climber 2.5–3 m (8–10 ft.) tall. Pruning group 2. Flowering from late spring to early summer and again in late summer. Single, greenish cream, well-formed flowers are 12–15 cm (4.75–6 in.)

Clematis 'Poulala' (Alabast). Photo by C. Chesshire.

wide with six to eight tepals. Flowers of the second flush are smaller at 9 cm (3.5 in.) wide. Best flower color in part shade. Shows up well against a dark background. Ideal for a small to medium-sized obelisk, trellis, or arbour. Grow with another clematis from pruning group 2 which has a contrasting flower color. Zones 4–9.

Clematis 'Praecox'

Herbaceous/Heracleifolia Group. RHS Award of Garden Merit (1993). Synonym: *C.* 'Jouiniana Praecox'. Hardy, vigorous, deciduous, semiherbaceous, non-clinging, 1.8–2.4 m (6–7.75 ft.) if grown supported, 0.9–1.2 m (3–4 ft.) tall and spreading up to 2.4 m (7.75 ft.) if allowed to scramble. Pruning group 3. Flowering from midsummer to early autumn. Single, pale mauve flowers comprise four, rarely five or six, narrow tepals, each up to 4 cm (1.5 in.) across and with a ridge along the margins. The tepals are deeper colored near the tips, which curve back upon themselves. Large, coarse leaves have serrated edges. Ideal for ground cover. Zones 3–9.

Clematis 'Prince Charles'

RHS Award of Garden Merit (2002). Hardy, moderately vigorous, compact, deciduous climber 1.8–2.4 m (6–7.75 ft.) tall. Very floriferous over a long period. Pruning group 3. Flowering from early summer to early autumn. Single, satiny midblue, semi-nodding flowers, 10 cm (4 in.) across, are composed of four to six broad but tapering, slightly twisting, deeply ribbed tepals. Suitable for any aspect except a north-facing one. Prone to mildew. May be cultivated short term in a container. Grow on an obelisk or trellis, or with a climbing rose. Looks well when allowed to grow over low-growing shrubs. Zones 4–9.

Clematis 'Princess Diana'

Texensis-Viorna Group. RHS Award of Garden Merit (2002). Synonyms: *C. texensis* 'Princess Diana', *C. texensis* 'The Princess of Wales'. Hardy, delightful, strong-growing, deciduous climber 1.8–2.4 m (6–7.75 ft.) tall. Normally herbaceous in habit with new shoots emerging from below ground level. Very floriferous when

Clematis 'Praecox'. Photo by R. Surman.

Clematis 'Prince Charles'. Photo by C. Chesshire.

established. Pruning group 3. Flowering from early summer to early autumn. Single, luminous pink, tulip-like flowers, 6 cm (2.25 in.) long, are composed of four tepals, each with a deeper pink bar and pointed tip, which recurves gently to make a trumpet-like shape as the flower matures. Outside of tepals boasts a distinctive bright pink color at the margins. Best in sun or

Clematis 'Princess Diana' with *Exochorda* ×*macrantha* 'The Bride'. Photo by M. Toomey.

part shade. New shoots at soil level need protection from slugs and snails. Grow through and over a low, wide shrub, preferably with silver foliage or prostrate conifers. Flowers will face upward. Zones 4–9.

Clematis 'Princess of Wales'

Hardy, moderately vigorous, deciduous climber 2.4–3 m (7.75–10 ft.) tall. Has a long flowering period. Pruning group 2. Flowering from early to late summer. Large, single, satiny, pale mauve, flat flowers, 15–20 cm (6–8 in.) across, with six to eight somewhat overlapping tepals, each wide at the middle but slightly tapering towards both ends. Each tepal carries central grooves shaded darker towards the basal half. Tepal tips are pointed. Suitable for a pergola, trellis, or medium-sized obelisk. Zones 4–9.

Clematis 'Prins Hendrik'

Trade name: Prince Hendrik. Hardy, moderately vigorous, compact, deciduous climber 1.8–2.4 m (6–7.75 ft.) tall. Pruning group 2. Flowering from late spring to midsummer. Single, lavender-blue flowers, 15–20 cm (6–8 in.) wide, carry six, sometimes seven, overlapping tepals with indented or notched margins. Each tepal has a deeply grooved central bar. Best in sun or part shade. Ideal for container culture. Suitable for a small to medium-sized obelisk or trellis. Zones 4–9.

Clematis 'Propertius'

Atragene Group. Hardy, moderately vigorous, deciduous climber 2.4–3 m (7.75–10 ft.) tall. Pruning group 1. Flowering from early to midspring. Double, pinkish mauve, nodding, slightly scented flowers, 7.5–9 cm (3–3.5 in.) across, are composed of four broad, spear-shaped tepals, each with three or four prominent ridges running from the base to the tip. There is much veining and crinkled texturing, and the coloring fades to silvery white at the margins. The outer tepals surround two layers of long, paler and narrower petal-like structures of similar length, which in turn surround an inner skirt of short pale cream

Clematis 'Princess of Wales'. Photo by C. Chesshire.

Clematis 'Prins Hendrik' (Prince Hendrik). Photo by R. Savill.

Clematis 'Propertius'. Photo by J. Lindmark.

staminodes tipped with green. Thrives in well-drained garden soils. Strongest flower scent in sun. Suitable for a medium-sized obelisk or trellis. Grow with other early flowering clematis or wall-trained shrubs which do not require heavy annual pruning. Zones 3–9.

Clematis 'Proteus'

Hardy, very vigorous, deciduous climber 1.8–2.4 m (6–7.75 ft.) tall. Pruning group 2. Flowering from late spring to early summer and again in late summer. Fully double, purple-pink flowers, 12.5–15 cm (5–6 in.) wide, are produced on old wood from the previous season. The outermost layer is composed of six broad yet pointed basal tepals, each with shades of pale green along the centre and a deeply textured surface. Inside this basal layer are successive layers of paler mauvish pink tepals, many of which are twisted with incurving margins and tips. Flowers of the second flush, produced on new growth of the current year, are single. Best in full or part sun. Requires protection from strong winds. Suitable for a small to medium-sized obelisk or trellis. Also suitable for short-term container culture. Team it with other wall-trained plants which do not require pruning. Zones 4–9.

Clematis 'Purpurea Plena Elegans'

Viticella Group. RHS Award of Garden Merit (1993). Synonym: *C. viticella* 'Purpurea Plena Elegans'. Hardy, deciduous climber 3–4 m (10–13 ft.) tall. Very vigorous when established. Pruning group 3. Flowering from midsummer to early autumn. Fully double, dark magenta, sterile flowers, 4.5–6 cm (1.75–2.25 in.) across, are carried on long stalks in rosettes. Each tepal recurves elegantly towards the tip and has a greyish tinge on its reverse side. Occasionally, the outer tepals may show green tips as the flowers open. With age the outer tepals wither and fall off, leaving the inner rows of tepals to open gradually over a period of time. Shows up well against a light background. Grow through a medium-sized tree, large shrub, or early flowering climbing rose. Suitable for an arch or pergola. Zones 3–9.

Clematis 'Proteus', with early, double flowers. Photo by C. Chesshire.

Clematis 'Proteus', with single flowers later in the season or in cold climates. Photo by J. Lindmark.

Clematis 'Purpurea Plena Elegans'. Photo by J. Lindmark.

Clematis recta. Photo by J. Lindmark.

Clematis recta

Herbaceous Group. Hardy, deciduous, clump-forming, not-too-erect, herbaceous perennial 1–2 m (3–6.5 ft.) tall. Has a long flowering period. Native to Europe and Russia. Pruning group 3. Flowering from early to late summer. Numerous, single, white, star-shaped flowers, 2–3 cm (0.75–1.25 in.) wide, are borne in large terminal flowerheads usually covering the upper half of the plant. The four tepals open wide and are slightly recurved. Some forms exude a strong hawthorn scent. Numerous seedheads are also attractive. Best in sun. If space permits, allow the flowering stems to flop on the ground, where they make an effective display. If trained on an artificial support, the stems will need tying-in. Zones 3–9.

Clematis recta 'Purpurea'

Herbaceous Group. Synonyms: *C*. 'Purpurea', *C. recta* var. *purpurea*. Hardy, deciduous, clump-forming, herbaceous perennial 0.9–1.8 m (3–6 ft.) tall. Pruning group 3. Flowering from early to late summer. Flowers similar to those of *C. recta*. This form is distinguished from the species by the purple leaves, which are distinctly dark and almost purple-bronze when young, turning green with age. White flowers contrast exceptionally well with the rich, dark foliage. Best in a sunny position. Zones 3–9.

Clematis 'Red Beetroot Beauty'

Atragene Group. Synonym: *C*. 'Betina'. Hardy, not-too-vigorous, compact, deciduous climber 1.8–2.4 m (6–7.75 ft.) tall. Pruning group 1. Flowering from early to midspring. Small, single, beet-red, bell-shaped, nodding flowers carry four, wide, spear-shaped, textured tepals, each 3.2 cm (1.25 in.) long. The tepals enclose an inner skirt of purple-tipped, pale white staminodes (sterile stamens). Best in well-drained garden soils enriched with humus. Ideal for container culture. May be trained on a small to medium-sized

Clematis recta 'Purpurea'. Photo by M. Toomey.

Clematis recta 'Purpurea', flowers. Photo by E. Leeds.

Clematis 'Red Beetroot Beauty'. Photo by J. Lindmark.

Clematis rehderiana. Photo by C. Chesshire.

obelisk or trellis. Allow to tumble over a low wall, where it looks splendid. Zones 3–9.

Clematis rehderiana

RHS Award of Garden Merit (1993). Hardy, very vigorous, scandent, woody, deciduous climber up to 7.7 m (25 ft.) tall and with an extensive spread. Native to western China. Pruning group 3. Flowering from midsummer to early autumn. Single, pale yellow, pendulous, bell-shaped, cowslip-scented flowers, 1.5–1.8 cm (0.5–0.75 in.) long, are borne in small groups on erect axillary and terminal clusters up to 23 cm (9 in.) long. Each flower is composed of four tepals which are longer than broad, velvety and hairy on the outer surface, smooth and hairless on the inner surface. The tepals reflex at the blunt tips just enough to expose the pale brownish yellow anthers carried on hairy, greenish cream filaments. Leaf-like bracts, similar in color to that of the tepals, often three-lobed and about 20 mm (0.75 in.) long, are a characteristic feature. Mature stems are ribbed and change from green to mauvish brown. Thrives in well-drained garden soils. Produces strongest scent in a sunny position. Suitable for a spacious wall or fence. Grow through medium-sized trees or large shrubs. Ideal for a large pergola. A good groundcover plant for a very large garden. Zones 6–9.

Clematis 'Rhapsody'

RHS Award of Garden Merit (2002). Hardy, moderately vigorous, deciduous climber, 2.4–3 m (7.75–10 ft.) tall. A beautiful free-flowering cultivar. Pruning group 3. Flowering from mid to late summer. Single, indigo blue flowers become intensely colored with age and are 10–12.5 cm (4–5 in.) across with four to six broad, pointed tepals. Best in sun or part shade. Avoid north-facing aspects. Grow with other climbing plants and roses. Train on a medium-sized obelisk or trellis. Suitable for short-term container culture. Zones 4–9.

Clematis 'Richard Pennell'

RHS Award of Garden Merit (1993). Hardy, moderately vigorous, deciduous climber 2.4–3 m (7.75–10 ft.) tall. A graceful cultivar. Pruning

Clematis 'Rhapsody'. Photo by C. Chesshire.

Clematis 'Richard Pennell'. Photo by C. Chesshire.

group 2. Flowering from late spring to early summer and again in late summer. Single, rosy purple-blue, well-formed flowers, 15–20 cm (6–8 in.) wide, carry six to eight saucer-shaped, overlapping tepals. Flower color tends to lose its lustre gradually with age. Partner it with climbing roses and other wall-trained shrubs which do not require severe pruning. Train up a medium-sized obelisk or trellis. Zones 4–9.

Clematis 'Roko-Kolla'

Hardy, moderately vigorous, deciduous, climber 1.5–2 m (5–6.5 ft.) tall. A late-flowering cultivar from Estonia. Pruning group 3. Flowering from midsummer to autumn. Single, white flowers tinged with yellow are 15–20 cm (6–8 in.) across and carry four to six gappy, pointed tepals, each with a pale yellow-green bar. Thrives in well-drained soils. Best in a sunny position. Suitable for a medium-sized obelisk or trellis. Zones 4–9.

Clematis 'Romantika'

British Clematis Society Certificate of Merit (1998). Hardy, moderately vigorous, deciduous climber 1.8–2.4 m (6–7.75 ft.) tall. Pruning group 3. Flowering from early to late summer. Single, very rich almost blackish purple, well-formed, firm flowers, 10–15 cm (4–6 in.) wide, are composed of four tepals, each heavily grooved along the centre and displaying a faint, lighter purple bar with age. Prone to mildew. Shows up well against a light background. Team it with a moderately vigorous shrub with either silver or golden leaves to show off the deep rich color. May be grown in a large container or trained on a small obelisk or trellis. Zones 3–9.

Clematis 'Rooguchi'

Hardy, vigorous, herbaceous, deciduous, non-climber 1.5–2 m (5–6.5 ft.) tall. A Japanese cultivar with a long flowering period. Pruning group 3. Flowering from early summer to au-

Clematis 'Roko-Kolla'. Photo by M. Toomey.

Clematis 'Romantika'. Photo by E. Leeds.

Clematis 'Rooguchi'. Courtesy of Ozawa Slide Library.

tumn. Single, velvety purple-violet, bell-shaped, nodding flowers, 5–7.5 cm (2–3 in.) across, are held on sturdy stalks. The four ribbed tepals are strongly recurved towards the tips and have expanded white margins. Best in a sunny position. May be prone to mildew in some locations. A splendid companion for a robust shrub boasting silver foliage. Train the stems up a trellis and tie them to the support at regular intervals. Zones 4–9.

Clematis 'Rosea'

Herbaceous/Integrifolia Group. RHS Award of Garden Merit (1993). Synonym: *C. integrifolia* 'Rosea'. Hardy, deciduous, non-clinging, herbaceous perennial 0.7–1.2 m (2.25–4 ft.) tall. A variable cultivar often propagated from seed. Beware of inferior seedlings. Best acquired from a reputable source. Pruning group 3. Flowering from early to late summer. Single, light pink to dark mauve-pink, bell-shaped, nodding, slightly scented flowers are borne on terminal shoots and in upper leaf axils. There are four pointed, prominently ribbed tepals, each 4–5 cm (1.5–2 in.) long. Deep coloring of pink is concentrated at the base of each tepal. Tepal margins of some forms slightly twisted, wavy, and covered in dense, short, and fine hairs. Best in garden soils enriched with humus. Suitable for any aspect but produces strongest scent in a sunny position. Place in the middle of an herbaceous border. Zones 3–9.

Clematis 'Rosy O'Grady'

Atragene Group. RHS Award of Garden Merit (2002). Hardy, vigorous, deciduous climber 3–4 m (10–13 ft.) tall. Pruning group 1. Flowering from mid to late spring and sporadically in summer. Semi-double, pinkish mauve, nodding flowers, 10–12 cm (4–4.75 in.) across, carry four nar-

Clematis 'Rosea'. Photo by R. Evison.

row tepals which are much longer than broad, each 5–7 cm (2–2.75 in.) long. Tepal margins tend to curve back upon themselves at a mid-point, giving a slightly twisted appearance. Outside of the tepal is darker than the inside and has dark pink veining from the base to the tip. Inner skirt of petal like sterile stamens is pale pinkish mauve and surrounds the pale yellow centre of fertile stamens. Best in well-drained garden soils. Suitable a pergola, medium-sized obelisk, or trellis in a small garden. Zones 3–9.

Clematis 'Rouge Cardinal'

Hardy, strong-growing, deciduous climber 1.8–2.4 m (6–7.75 ft.) tall. Pruning group 3. Flowering profusely from early to late summer. Single, velvety red flowers, 10–13 cm (4–5 in.) wide, are borne abundantly and carry six rounded yet pointed, slightly recurved tepals, giving the flower a very full and rounded appearance. Shows up well against a light background. May be grown through a medium-sized shrub or climbing rose. Suitable for short-term container culture. Zones 4–9.

Clematis 'Royal Velours'

Viticella Group. RHS Award of Garden Merit (1993). Synonym: *C. viticella* 'Royal Velours'. Hardy, moderately vigorous, deciduous climber 2.5–3 m (8–10 ft.) tall or taller. Pruning group 3. Flowering from early summer to autumn. Single, velvety dark reddish purple to reddish black, semi-nodding flowers are 6–8 cm (2.25–3.25 in.) wide and composed of four to six overlapping tepals which are deeply veined with lighter midribs. Shows up well against a light background or in sunlight. Most effective when grown through shrubs with silver, grey, or golden foliage, and with climbing roses. Zones 3–9.

Clematis 'Royalty'

RHS Award of Garden Merit (1993). Hardy, moderately vigorous, compact, deciduous climber 1.8–2.4 m (6–7.75 ft.) tall. Pruning group 2. Flowering from late spring to early summer and again in early autumn. Double, rich blue-mauve flowers, 10–15 cm (4–6 in.) wide,

Clematis 'Rosy O'Grady'. Photo by C. Chesshire.

Clematis 'Rouge Cardinal'. Photo by J. Lindmark.

Clematis 'Royal Velours'. Photo by J. Lindmark.

are produced on old wood of the previous season. They are composed of a row of eight or nine overlapping, rounded basal tepals, each with a pale mauve bar overlaid with dark purple veins along the centre. Subsequent inner layers of shorter tepals boast similar coloring. Flowers of the second flush are single, borne on new growth from the current season. Best in full or part sun. Requires a sheltered position to prevent wind damage to the flowers. Train it up a small obelisk or trellis. Suitable for short-term container culture. Zones 4–9.

Clematis 'Royalty'. Photo by C. Chesshire.

Clematis 'Ruby'

Atragene Group. Synonym: *C. alpina* 'Ruby'. Hardy, vigorous, deciduous climber rapidly growing 2.5–3 m (8–10 ft.) tall. Extremely floriferous. Pruning group 1. Flowering from mid to late spring. Single, dusky mauvish red, slightly nodding flowers with four tepals, each 4–5 cm (1.5–2 in.) long. Thrives in sharply drained soils. If planted in a sunny position will give some flowers in late summer. Also produces vibrant flower color in sun, although it is useful for north-and east-facing aspects. Best in sharply drained soils. Regular thinning out of the well-established plant is essential. Suitable for a pergola or wall. May be teamed with a robust, large shrub. Zones 3–9.

Clematis 'Rüütel'

Hardy, moderately vigorous, compact, deciduous climber to 1.8 m (6 ft.) tall. Floriferous. Pruning group 3. Flowering from mid to late summer. Sin-

Clematis 'Ruby'. Photo by J. Lindmark.

gle, crimson flowers, 13–15 cm (5–6 in.) in diameter, carry six to eight tepals, each deeply grooved in the middle. Suitable for a small obelisk or a large container. May be grown with a small shrub. Zones 4–9.

Clematis 'Saturn'

Hardy, moderately vigorous, deciduous climber 2.4–3 m (7.75–10 ft.) tall. Pruning group 2. Flowering from mid to late spring and again in late summer. Large, single, lavender-blue flowers, 13–15 cm (5–6 in.) across, are borne freely and carry six to eight tepals, each with a light mauve bar along the centre. Suitable for a medium-sized obelisk or trellis. May be trained through other wall-trained plants which do not require severe pruning. Zones 4–9.

Clematis 'Scartho Gem'

Hardy, moderately vigorous, compact, deciduous climber 1.8–2.4 m (6–7.75 ft.) tall. Pruning group 2. Flowering from late spring to early summer and again in late summer. Semi-double, pink-cochineal flowers, 15–20 cm (6–8 in.) across, are borne on old growth from the previous season and consist of six to eight broad, overlapping tepals, each with a deeper colored band along the centre and with gently scalloped margins. Flowers of the second flush, borne on new growth of the current season, are single, paler colored, and smaller at 15 cm (6 in.) across. Suitable for a medium-sized obelisk or trellis. May be grown through a medium-sized shrub which does not require severe pruning. Zones 4–9.

Clematis 'Sealand Gem'

Hardy, not-too-vigorous, deciduous climber 2.4–3 m (7.75–10 ft.) tall. Not floriferous. Pruning group 2. Flowering from late spring to early summer and again in early autumn. Single, satiny mauvish blue flowers, 13 cm (5 in.) wide, appear to be semi-double and do not open out fully or flat. Six to eight blunt, overlapping, twisted tepals have irregularly wavy margins. Each tepal has a reddish pink central bar. Suitable for a medium-sized obelisk, trellis, arch, or pergola. Grow with

Clematis 'Rüütel'. Photo by J. Lindmark.

Clematis 'Saturn'. Photo by C. Chesshire.

Clematis 'Scartho Gem'. Photo by C. Chesshire.

Clematis 'Sealand Gem'. Photo by E. Leeds.

Clematis 'Silver Moon'. Photo by M. Toomey.

a small to medium-sized, moderately vigorous shrub which does not require annual pruning. Zones 4–9.

Clematis 'Silver Moon'

Hardy, very vigorous, strong-growing, deciduous climber 2.4–3 m (7.75–10 ft.) tall. Has a long flowering season. Pruning optional, group 2, or group 3. A hard pruning (group 3) results in the loss of early flowers. Flowering from late spring to early autumn. Single, satiny mother-of-pearl grey flowers are 10–15 cm (4–6 in.) wide with six to eight overlapping, blunt tepals. Produces best flowers in part shade or a north-facing aspect. Grow on a medium-sized trellis, obelisk, pergola, or arch. May be teamed with a medium-sized shrub which does not require annual pruning. Zones 4–9.

Clematis 'Sinee Dozhd'

Herbaceous Group. Trade name: Blue Rain. Hardy, very vigorous, semi-herbaceous, non-clinging, shrubby perennial 1.2–1.8 m (3.5–6 ft.) tall. Very floriferous with a long flowering period. Pruning group 3. Flowering from early to late

Clematis 'Sinee Dozhd' (Blue Rain). Photo by C. Chesshire.

summer. Single, violet-blue, bell-shaped, nodding, slightly fragrant flowers, 5 cm (2 in.) across, carry four tepals, each 3.5 cm (1.25 in.) long and 1.5 cm (0.5 in.) wide. Broad at and above the midpoint and tapering towards the base, the tepals boast some purple coloring along the middle and pale blue along the margins. If trained on an artificial support, the stems will need tying-in. Best effect when allowed to grow through a tall shrub with golden foliage. Zones 4–9.

Clematis 'Sir Trevor Lawrence'

Texensis-Viorna Group. Synonym: *C. texensis* 'Sir Trevor Lawrence'. Hardy, deciduous climber 2.5–3 m (8–10 ft.) tall. Normally herbaceous in habit with new shoots emerging from below ground level. Pruning group 3. Flowering from midsummer to early autumn. Single, dark purple-red, tulip-like flowers, 5 cm (2 in.) long, carry four pointed tepals, each with a scarlet central bar. The outer surface is whitish pink to reddish pink depending on exposure to sunshine. Deep pink veins extend along the length of the tepals. As the flower matures, the tepal tips recurve. Best in sun or part shade. Prone to mildew. New shoots at soil level need protection from slugs and snails. Grow over groundcover shrubs, prostrate conifers, or a low wall where the upright, well-held flowers can be appreciated. Train as a specimen plant on a small to medium-sized obelisk or trellis. Shows up well against a light background. Zones 4–9.

Clematis 'Sir Trevor Lawrence'. Photo by E. Leeds.

Clematis 'Snow Queen'

Hardy, moderately vigorous, compact, deciduous climber 1.8–2.4 m (6–7.75 ft.) tall. Pruning group 2. Flowering from late spring to early summer and again in late summer. Single, mauve pinkish flowers, 15–18 cm (6–7 in.) across, carry six to eight overlapping, pointed tepals, each with a textured, deeply ribbed surface giving a rippled effect, and each tapering to a blunt tip. Flowers of the second flush are a pinky white, later fading to pure white. Excellent against a dark background. Suitable for a medium-sized obelisk or trellis. Ideal for short-term container culture. Grow through a wall-trained shrub. Zones 4–9.

Clematis 'Snow Queen'. Photo by M. Toomey.

Clematis 'Södertälje'

Viticella Group. Synonym: *C. viticella* 'Södertälje'. Hardy, strong-growing, deciduous climber 3–4 m (10–13 ft.) tall. Pruning group 3. Flowering from midsummer to early autumn. Single, pinkish red, semi-nodding, gappy flowers, 5–7.5 cm (2–3 in.) across, are borne profusely and are composed of four to six tepals with recurving tips. Tepals of early flowers tend to be green but coloring disappears as the season progresses and normal color is restored. Best in sun or part shade. Ideal for growing through medium-sized trees and large, open shrubs such as rhododendrons. Zones 3–9.

Clematis 'Södertälje'. Photo by J. Lindmark.

Clematis 'Souvenir du Capitaine Thuilleaux'

Synonym: *C.* 'Capitaine Thuilleaux'. Hardy, moderately vigorous, compact, deciduous climber 1.8–2.4 m (6–7.75 ft.) tall. Pruning group 2. Flowering from late spring to early summer and again from late summer to early autumn. Large, single, pale pink-grey flowers are 15–20 cm (6–8 in.) wide and carry six to eight overlapping, pointed tepals, each with a broad strawberry-pink central bar. Best in part shade to prevent flower color from fading. Grow up and over moderately vigorous shrubs which do not require annual pruning. May also be allowed to clamber through wall-trained shrubs or small fruit trees. Ideal for short-term container culture. Zones 4–9.

Clematis 'Souvenir du Capitaine Thuilleaux'. Courtesy British Clematis Society Slide Library.

Clematis 'Special Occasion'. Photo by E. Leeds.

Clematis stans. Photo by J. Lindmark.

Clematis 'Special Occasion'

Hardy, not-too-vigorous, compact, free-flowering, deciduous climber 1.5–1.8 m (5–6 ft.) tall. Pruning group 2. Flowering from late spring to late summer. Single, pale bluish pink flowers are borne on short growths and composed of six to eight rounded tepals, each with lighter coloring along the centre and distinguished by pronounced ribbing. Ideal for container culture. Suitable for growing up and over small to medium-size prostrate shrubs which do not require annual pruning. May also be teamed with low-growing conifers. Zones 4–9.

Clematis stans

Herbaceous Group. Hardy, deciduous, non-clinging, woody-based, herbaceous subshrub 0.9–1.2 m (3–4 ft.) tall. Has a long flowering period. Native to Japan. Pruning group 3. Flowering from midsummer to early autumn. Single, tubular, hy-acinth-like flowers, 2–2.5 cm (0.75–1 in.) long, are borne in abundance on branched stalks and are hairy on the outside. Flower color varies from plant to plant and is very pale blue to almost white to pale lavender-blue with a paler centre. The four pointed tepals strongly recurve with age. Some clones have very congested flower heads, others more open. Some forms are scented. Male, female, or hermaphrodite flowers may be on the same or separate plants. Best in soils with good drainage and some moisture. Young plants may require staking. Plant towards the back of a mixed or herbaceous border. Zones 4–9.

Clematis 'Star of India'

RHS First Class Certificate (1867), RHS Award of Garden Merit (1993). Hardy, vigorous, deciduous climber 3–3.6 m (10–11.5 ft.) tall. Pruning group 3. Flowering from midsummer to early autumn. Single, reddish plum to violet-purple flowers, 10–12.5

Clematis 'Star of India'. Photo by J. Lindmark.

cm (4–5 in.) across, carry four to six textured tepals with rounded edges. Each tepal boasts a cerise central bar from which reddish veins radiate. Prone to mildew. Grow through a medium-sized to large shrub. Ideal for a pergola, obelisk, or arbour. Team it with a climbing rose or another clematis in the same pruning group. Zones 4–9.

Clematis 'Sunset'

RHS Award of Garden Merit (2002). Hardy, moderately vigorous, compact, deciduous climber 1.8–2.4 m (6–7.75 ft.) tall. Pruning group 2. Flowering from early to late summer. Single, deep reddish purple-pink flowers, 10–12.5 cm (4–5 in.) wide, are borne very freely. The six to eight lightly textured tepals taper towards the tips and boast a satiny cerise central bar. Ideal for a small to medium-sized obelisk or trellis. Partner it with a medium-sized shrub which requires little or no pruning. Suitable for short-term container culture. Zones 4–9.

Clematis 'Sylvia Denny'

Hardy, moderately vigorous, compact, deciduous climber 1.8–2.4 m (6–7.75 ft.) tall. Pruning group 2. Flowering from late spring to early summer and again from late summer to early autumn. Semi-double, white, neatly formed, camellia-like flowers are 10–12.5 cm (4–5-in.) wide and are borne on old wood of the previous season. A distinguishing feature is the absence of any greening in the tepals. Flowers of the second flush, produced on new growth of the current season, are single. Suitable for full or part sun. Requires protection from strong winds. Shows up best against a dark background. Grow on a small to medium-sized obelisk or trellis. Ideal for container culture. Zones 4–9.

Clematis 'Tage Lundell'

Atragene Group. Hardy, moderately vigorous, deciduous climber 2.5–3 m (8–10 ft.) tall. Pruning group 1. Flowering from mid to late spring.

Clematis 'Sunset'. Photo by C. Chesshire.

Clematis 'Sylvia Denny'.
Photo by V. Denny.

Clematis 'Tage Lundell'.
Photo by R. Surman.

Single, dark plum purple flowers carry four tepals, each 4–5 cm (1.5–2 in.) long. The tepals surround an inner skirt of mauvish pink petal-like structures (sterile stamens), which confer a double appearance on the flower. Best in sharply drained soils. Suitable for any aspect, including cold, windy ones. A useful plant for a small garden. Attractive on a pergola or trellis. May be allowed to roam into medium-sized trees or large shrubs which do not require annual pruning. Zones 3–9.

Clematis 'Tango'

Viticella Group. Synonym: *C. viticella* 'Tango'. Hardy, vigorous, deciduous climber 3–4 m (10–13 ft.) tall. Pruning group 3. Flowering from midsummer to early autumn. Single, white, somewhat rounded flowers, 5 cm (2 in.) across, are composed of four or five tepals, each with wide crimson margins and with deep pink veining towards the centre from the sides and down the midrib. Grow naturally through a medium-sized tree, large shrub, or climbing rose. Suitable for a large pergola, obelisk, or trellis. Ideal for growing with spring-flowering plants, thus bringing later-flowering interest and color. Zones 3–9.

Clematis tangutica

Tangutica Group. Synonym: *C. orientalis* var. *tangutica*. Hardy, vigorous, deciduous climber to 6 m (20 ft.) tall or taller. Has a long flowering period. Native to northwestern China, Tibet, northern India, and Mongolia. Pruning group 3. Flowering from early to late summer. Single, golden yellow, solitary, pendulous, bell- to lantern-shaped flowers with a silky sheen are not fully open. They consist of four pointed, very slightly spreading tepals, each 2.5–4 cm (1–1.5 in.) long, with small hairs on the outside, smooth and shiny inside. Attractive seedheads are produced from autumn through winter. Thrives in sharply drained soils. Best in sun or part shade. Grow through a medium-sized to large shrub, tree, or conifer. Useful for covering expansive wall spaces. May be grown to form mounds of foliage, flowers, and seedheads at ground level, in large gardens. Suitable for a large pergola or free-standing trellis. Zones 4–9.

Clematis 'Tango'. Photo by E. Leeds.

Clematis tangutica. Photo by J. Lindmark.

Clematis 'Tartu'. Photo by V. Miettinen.

Clematis 'Tentel'. Photo by E. Leeds.

Clematis terniflora. Photo by E. Leeds.

Clematis 'Tartu'

Hardy, moderately vigorous, compact, deciduous climber 1.5–1.8 m (5–6 ft.) tall. A cultivar with a long flowering period. Pruning group 2. Flowering from late spring to early summer and again in late summer. Single, bluish purple flowers, 10–15 cm (4–6 in.) wide, carry four to six overlapping, pointed tepals with wavy margins. May be grown in containers. Suitable for a small obelisk or trellis. Zones 4–9.

Clematis 'Tentel'

Hardy, not-too-vigorous, compact, deciduous climber 1.8–2.4 m (6–7.75 ft.) tall. Pruning group 3. Flowering from mid to late summer. Single, rosy lavender flowers, 5–8 cm (2–3.25 in.) across, are formed of six overlapping, pointed tepals with frilly, serrated margins. A central bar running down each tepal from the base to the tip is a lighter shade. Reverse side of the tepal has a prominently ribbed rose bar. Best in garden soils enriched with humus. Allow to tumble over a low wall. Partner it with a moderately vigorous climbing rose. Zones 3–9.

Clematis terniflora
Sweet autumn clematis

Synonym: *C. maximowicziana*. Hardy, strong-growing, vigorous, deciduous (sometimes semi-evergreen) climber to 10 m (33 ft.) tall or taller. Native to China, Taiwan, Korea, and Japan. Pruning group 3. Flowering from late summer to mid-autumn. Single, white, star-like, hawthorn-scented flowers, 1.5–3 cm (0.5–1.25 in.) across, are borne in large clusters in the leaf axils on new growth of the current year. Four narrow tepals, longer than broad and spreading widely apart, are hairy on the outside. Grooved stems are hairy when young and become semi-woody with age. Best in well-drained garden soils. Prefers a dry site. Must have a warm to hot location with plenty of sunshine to flower well. Does exceptionally well in the gardens of eastern United States. Not for very cold and exposed gardens. Suitable for covering a warm, south-facing wall or fence. Allow it to scramble into medium-sized to large trees or shrubs. Zones 5–9.

Clematis 'The President'

RHS Award of Garden Merit (1993). Hardy, moderately vigorous, deciduous climber 2.4–3 m (7.75–10 ft.) tall. An extremely popular cultivar. Pruning group 2. Flowering from late spring to early summer and again from late summer to early autumn. Single, rich purple-blue, somewhat cupped flowers, 15–17 cm (6–7 in.) across, carry six to eight overlapping, pointed tepals with undulating margins and silvery undersides. Leaves are bronzy when young, becoming dark green with age. Ideal against a pillar or on a pergola, arch, large trellis, or obelisk. A companion for a large shrub with silver or golden foliage which does not require severe pruning or regular clipping. Not for a container. Zones 4–9.

Clematis 'The Vagabond'

Hardy, moderately vigorous, compact, deciduous climber 1.5–1.8 m (5–6 ft.) tall. Pruning group 2. Flowering from late spring to early summer and again from late summer to early autumn. Single flowers, at first very deep purple, almost black, when fully opened, shading to crimson at the centre, are 13–15 cm (5–6 in.) across and composed of six, sometimes eight, pointed tepals with undulating margins. May be grown in a large container for a season or two. Train it up a small obelisk or trellis. Zones 4–9.

Clematis tibetana subsp. *vernayi* 'Orange Peel'

Tangutica Group. RHS Award of Merit (1950). Synonym: *C.* 'Orange Peel'. Hardy, moderately vigorous, deciduous climber to 5 m (16 ft.) tall. Several forms are in cultivation, probably grown from seed, with varying color and form. Pruning group 3. Partial pruning is recommended. This involves pruning half the vines down to just above the lowest pair of live buds and the other half to

Clematis 'The President'. Photo by E. Leeds.

Clematis 'The Vagabond'. Photo by C. Chesshire.

Clematis tibetana subsp. vernayi 'Orange Peel' Photo by C. Chesshire.

autumn. Single, white, open flowers, 10 cm (4 in.) wide, carry five or six tepals, with deep purple veining becoming more intense towards the incurved margins. Suitable for sun or part shade. Grow through a large shrub or conifer with silvery or golden foliage. Partner it with a climbing rose. Train on a trellis or an obelisk. Allow to scramble over golden heathers and prostrate conifers. Zones 3–9.

Clematis 'Victoria'

RHS First Class Certificate (1870), RHS Award of Garden Merit (2002). Hardy, vigorous, strong-growing, deciduous climber 3–3.6 m (10–11.5 ft.) tall. A popular cultivar. Pruning group 3. Flowering from midsummer to early autumn. Single, reddish mauve, well-formed flowers are 14 cm (5.5 in.) across and are composed of four to six, overlapping, pointed yet wide, textured tepals with slightly notched margins. Each tepal has a shading of rose-pink along the centre, the color fading to light mauve by tepal fall. May be prone to mildew in sheltered locations. Shows up well against a light background. Ideal for growing naturally through other shrubs and climbers. Suitable for a pergola, arbour, or large obelisk. Zones 4–9.

Clematis 'Ville de Lyon'

Hardy, vigorous, strong-growing, deciduous climber 3–3.6 m (10–11.5 ft.) tall. A well-known, widely grown, and free-flowering cultivar with a long flowering season. Pruning group 3. If left unpruned, ripened old stems produce early flowers. Flowering from early summer to early autumn. Single, velvety, cherry red flowers, 10–15 cm (4–6 in.) wide, with six, overlapping, neatly formed, rounded tepals. The tepals have blunt tips, and both the tips and margins are slightly recurving. Each tepal has a wide, deep pink central bar and pink veins. Grow through large shrubs or conifers as the older leaves at the base of this cultivar tend to go brown and are best hidden. Zones 4–9.

Clematis 'Viola'

Hardy, moderately vigorous, deciduous climber 2.4–3 m (7.75–10 ft.) tall. Pruning group 3.

Clematis 'Victoria'. Photo by C. Chesshire.

Clematis 'Ville de Lyon'. Photo by C. Chesshire.

Clematis 'Viola' growing through *Abies lasiocarpa* (alpine fir). Photo by J. Lindmark.

Flowering from mid to late summer. Single, deep bluish violet flowers, 10–14 cm (4–5.5 in.) wide, are freely produced and carry five or six short, broad tepals with gently notched margins. Ideal for very cold gardens. Grow naturally through large shrubs or small trees, or on a pergola, obelisk, or trellis. Zones 4–9.

Clematis 'Violet Purple'

Atragene Group. Hardy, moderately vigorous, deciduous climber 2.4–3 m (7.75–10 ft.) tall. A very fine, undemanding Swedish cultivar with elegant flowers. Pruning group 3. Flowering from mid to late spring, and occasionally from midsummer onwards. Single, violet-purple, nodding flowers

Clematis 'Violet Purple' with *C. turkestanica*, a Himalayan plant closely related to *C. alpina*. Photo by J. Lindmark.

are composed of four somewhat elongated tepals, each 5–5.5 cm (2–2.25 in.) long with margins curled back upon themselves at midpoint and gently at the tips. The leaves are not very crowded on the stem, thus enabling the flowers to be viewed easily. Best in well-drained garden soils. Grow as a specimen plant cascading over the wall of a raised bed or trained on a trellis or other suitable support. Zones 3–9.

Clematis viorna
Leather flower, vase vine

Texensis-Viorna Group. Hardy, woody-based, herbaceous, deciduous scrambler or subshrub

Clematis viorna. Photo by E. Leeds.

Clematis viticella. Photo by J. Lindmark.

1.8–2.4 m (6–7.75 ft.) tall. Native to eastern United States. Pruning group 3. Flowering from midsummer to early autumn. Small, single, pale lavender to reddish purple, urn-shaped, strongly ribbed, nodding flowers, 2.5–4 cm (1–1.5 in.) long, carry four pointed, recurving, thick, leathery tepals, which are pale yellow towards their smooth, woolly tips. Tepal margins are densely covered in short, fine, greyish white hairs, giving a cottony matted appearance. Seedheads are large and spectacular. Achene bodies are prominently rimmed and somewhat hairy, and the seedtails are feathery, light yellow or brownish, spreading or coiled loosely. Terminal leaflets end in a slender tendril-like structure. Best in sharply drained soils. Protect new shoots at soil level from slugs and snails. Grow through low shrubs and low walls, where the small flowers can be enjoyed at close quarters. Ideal as a specimen plant in a container. Zones 4–9.

Clematis viticella

Viticella Group. RHS Award of Garden Merit (2002). Hardy, vigorous, deciduous climber 3–5 m (10–16 ft.) tall. Native to Turkey and Italy. Pruning group 3. Flowering from mid to late summer. Single, blue-violet, nodding, bell-shaped flowers, 3–5 cm (1.25–2 in.) wide, are produced in abundance on new wood of the current season. There are four tepals. Inside margins of the tepals are dark blue. Inside of tepals is dark blue at the margins with a paler bar down the centre and darker veining. Outside of tepals is paler and has a greyer appearance. Grow through a small to medium-sized tree or a large shrub. Train on a trellis or pergola. Partner it with early flowering climbing roses. Zones 3–9.

Clematis viticella 'Flore Pleno'

Viticella Group. Synonyms: *C. viticella* 'Mary Rose', *C.* 'Purpurea Plena'. Hardy, deciduous climber 3–4 m (10–13 ft.) tall. Vigorous when established. A very old plant with an interesting history and brought back into cultivation in 1982. Pruning group 3. Flowering from midsummer to early autumn. Small, double, smoky amethyst, sterile flowers, 4–5 cm (1.5–2 in.) wide, are pro-

Clematis viticella 'Flore Pleno'. Photo by J. Lindmark.

Clematis viticella 'Lisboa'. Photo by J. Lindmark.

duced in profusion in rosettes and give a spiky appearance. Suitable for sun or part shade. Shows up well against a white or light background, such as a wall or through a medium-sized to large conifer or a tree with golden or grey foliage. Not recommended for a garden with limited space. Zones 3–9.

Clematis viticella 'Lisboa'

Viticella Group. Synonym: *C. campaniflora* 'Lisboa'. Hardy, moderately vigorous, deciduous climber 2.4–3.6 m (7.75–11.5 ft.) tall. Raised in the Lisbon University Botanic Garden, Portugal. Pruning group 3. Flowering from early to late summer.

Clematis 'Vostok'.
Photo by E. Leeds.

Clematis 'Vyvyan
Pennell'. Photo by
C. Chesshire.

Clematis 'W. E.
Gladstone'. Photo by
C. Chesshire.

Single, mauvish blue, bell-shaped, nodding flowers are 5 cm (2 in.) across. The four pointed tepals, longer than broad, with wavy margins, open wide and are recurved in the upper third. A handsome climber for a large pergola, obelisk, or trellis. May be grown up and over large shrubs or medium-sized trees. Zones 3–9.

Clematis 'Vostok'

British Clematis Society Certificate of Merit (2000). Hardy, moderately vigorous, deciduous climber 2.4–3 m (7.75–10 ft.) tall. Pruning group 3. Flowering from mid to late summer. Single, reddish purple flowers are 10–15 cm (4–6 in.) wide and composed of four to six tepals with deep red veins and a central bar. The tepals tend to recurve at the margins and tips and are sometimes twisted. Grow through a prostrate conifer or large shrub, or on a pergola, trellis, or large obelisk. Zones 4–9.

Clematis 'Vyvyan Pennell'

RHS Award of Garden Merit (1993). Hardy, vigorous, deciduous climber 1.8–3 m (6–10 ft.) tall. Very strong-growing when established. Pruning group 2. Flowering from late spring to early summer and again in early autumn. Fully double, pinkish to mauvish purple flowers with hints of red are 15–18 cm (6–7 in.) wide and are produced on old wood of the previous season. Six to 10 somewhat broad and overlapping basal tepals surround subsequent layers of shorter, pointed, rosy lavender tepals. Flowers of the second flush, produced on new growth of the current season, are single and colored a deep lilac-mauve. Best in sun or part shade, in a frost-free position. Requires protection from strong winds. Tends to flower early. Can be susceptible to clematis wilt when young. Suitable for a pergola, arbour, medium-sized to large obelisk, or trellis. Grow through a small tree or large shrub not requiring annual pruning. Zones 4–9.

Clematis 'W. E. Gladstone'

Hardy, strong-growing, deciduous climber 3–3.6 m (10–11.5 ft.) tall. Has a long flowering period.

Pruning optional, group 2, or group 3. A hard pruning (group 3) results in the loss of early flowers. Flowering from early summer to early autumn. Single, midblue to pale blue flowers are 20–25 cm (8–10 in.) wide and carry six or seven broad yet pointed tepals, each with rose pink shading along the centre in young flowers that fades with age. Suitable for sun or part shade. Requires a sheltered position to prevent wind damage to the large flowers. Grow on an arbour, pergola, large obelisk, or trellis. Zones 4–9.

Clematis 'Wada's Primrose'

Synonym: *C.* 'Manshuu-ki'. Hardy, not-too-vigorous, compact, deciduous climber 1.8–2.4 m (6–7.75 ft.) tall. Pruning group 2. Flowering from late spring to early summer and again in late summer. Large, single, primrose-yellow flowers, 15–17 cm (6–7 in.) across, are formed of eight overlapping tepals, each broader in the middle and tapering smartly to a point, with the deepest color concentrated along centrally placed stripes. Attractive, spherical seedheads remain on the plant for a long period. Stems are somewhat thin and weak. Best in part shade to preserve flower color. Suitable for short-term container culture. Grow on a small obelisk or trellis with another moderately vigorous, bushy climber or a small to medium-sized open shrub which does not require severe annual pruning. Zones 4–9.

Clematis 'Wada's Primrose'. Photo by J. Lindmark.

Clematis 'Warszawska Nike' (Midnight Showers). Photo by S. Marczyński.

Clematis 'Warszawska Nike'

RHS Award of Garden Merit (2002). Trade name: Midnight Showers. Hardy, moderately vigorous, compact, deciduous climber 1.8–2.4 m (6–7.75 ft.) tall. Pruning group 3. Flowering from mid-summer to early autumn. Single, rich, velvety reddish purple flowers are 12.5–15 cm (5–6 in.) wide and carry six to eight overlapping tepals, each one deeply grooved along the centre. Tepal margins are gently scalloped, and the reverse of the tepals is shaded silvery. Shows up well against a light background, such as shrubs or medium-sized trees which have light-colored leaves. Suitable for a medium-sized obelisk or trellis. Zones 4–9.

Clematis 'Westerplatte'

Hardy, compact, slender, deciduous climber 1–1.8 m (3–6 ft.) tall. A delightful Polish cultivar with a long flowering period. Pruning optional, group 2, or group 3. A hard pruning (group 3) results in the loss of early flowers. Flowering from late spring to late summer. Single, rich, dark velvety red flowers, 10–12.5 cm (4–5 in.) wide, carry 8 to 10 broad, rounded, well-formed, overlapping tepals, which have gaps between them at the point of origination near the central boss. Tepal tips are recurved. Excellent for container culture. Grow up and over a moderately vigorous shrub with light green or golden leaves. Suitable for a small obelisk or trellis. Zones 4–9.

Clematis 'Will Goodwin'

RHS Award of Garden Merit (1993). Moderately vigorous, deciduous climber 2.4–3 m (7.75–10 ft.) tall. Has a long flowering period. Pruning group 2. Flowering from early summer to early autumn. Single, lavender-blue flowers, 15–18 cm (6–7 in.) wide, fade to light blue with age and carry six to eight overlapping, tapering tepals with deeply notched margins. Train it up a large obelisk or trellis. Suitable for a pergola or arbour. May be teamed with another medium to large shrub which requires little or no pruning. Zones 4–9.

Clematis 'William Kennett'

An easy-to-grow plant. Hardy, vigorous, strong-growing, deciduous climber 3–3.6 m (10–11.5

Clematis 'Westerplatte'. Photo by S. Marczyński.

Clematis 'Will Goodwin'. Photo by C. Chesshire.

Clematis 'William Kennett'. Photo by M. Brown.

Clematis 'Willy'. Photo by R. Surman.

ft.) tall. Pruning group 2. Flowering from early to midsummer and again in early autumn. A profusion of single, satiny mauvish blue flowers, 15–20 cm (6–8 in.) wide. Six to eight broad but tapering, overlapping, and ribbed tepals have undulating margins. Rose-pink shadings diffuse from the centre of each tepal along each rib and fade gradually. Grow on an arbour, arch, pergola, large obelisk, or trellis. Zones 4–9.

Clematis 'Willy'

Atragene Group. Hardy, moderately vigorous, deciduous climber 2–3 m (6.5–10 ft.) tall. Floriferous and charming. Pruning group 1. Flowering from mid to late spring, with some flowers from mid to late summer. Single, pale rose-pink, nodding flowers, about 10 cm (4 in.) wide, are produced on short shoots from the previous season's old wood. The four tepals, each 4–5 cm (1.5–2

in.) long, are slightly darker on the outside and distinctly veined. Staminodes are white. Best in well-drained soil. Ideal for a small garden. Suitable for an arch or pergola. Zones 4–9.

Clematis 'Yukikomachi'

Hardy, moderately vigorous, compact, deciduous climber 1.8–2.4 m (6–7.75 ft.) tall. Pruning group 2. Flowering from late spring to early summer and again in late summer. Single, pale lavender flowers, 15–20 cm (6–8 in.) across, carry six broad yet pointed, slightly cupped tepals which overlap near the base. Each tepal has a central bar of white which fades into the textured surface. Tips of tepals are frequently tinged yellowish brown. Best in part shade to preserve flower color. May be grown in container for a season or two. Suitable for growing on a small obelisk or trellis. Zones 4–9.

Clematis 'Yukikomachi'. Photo by M. Humphries.

Clematis 'Zoin' (Inspiration). Photo by S. Marczyński.

Clematis 'Zoin'

Herbaceous/Integrifolia Group. Trade name: Inspiration. Hardy, deciduous plant with herbaceous stems to 1.8 m (6 ft.) tall or slightly taller. Very floriferous. Pruning group 3. Flowering from early summer to early autumn. Single, deep pink, somewhat erect and outward-facing flowers, 5–8 cm (2–3 in.) wide, are held on medium to long stalks. The four, occasionally five, tepals are wider towards the top and pointed, with wavy margins. Best in garden soils enriched with humus. Team it with a climbing rose or medium-sized shrub. May be trained on an obelisk, trellis, or arch. Zones 4–9.

USDA HARDINESS ZONE MAP

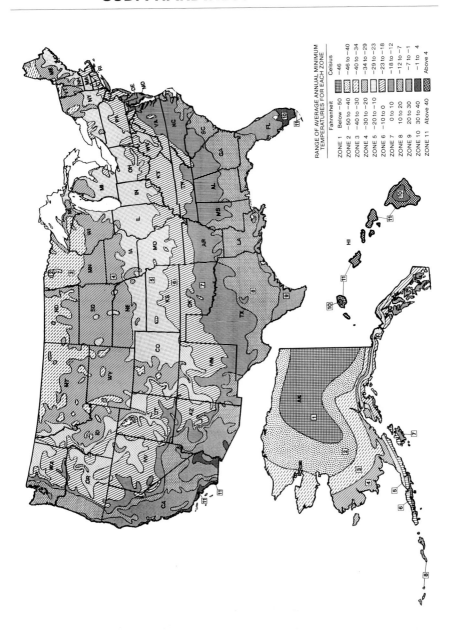

RANGE OF AVERAGE ANNUAL MINIMUM TEMPERATURES FOR EACH ZONE		
	Fahrenheit	Celsius
ZONE 1	Below −50	−46
ZONE 2	−50 to −40	−46 to −40
ZONE 3	−40 to −30	−40 to −34
ZONE 4	−30 to −20	−34 to −29
ZONE 5	−20 to −10	−29 to −23
ZONE 6	−10 to 0	−23 to −18
ZONE 7	0 to 10	−18 to −12
ZONE 8	10 to 20	−12 to −7
ZONE 9	20 to 30	−7 to −1
ZONE 10	30 to 40	−1 to 4
ZONE 11	Above 40	Above 4

EUROPEAN HARDINESS ZONE MAP

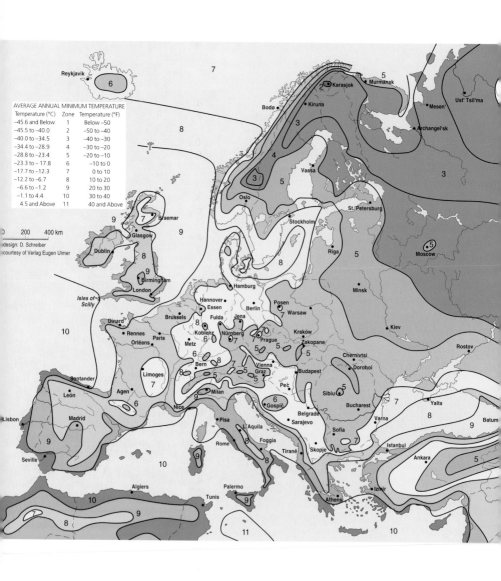

AVERAGE ANNUAL MINIMUM TEMPERATURE

Temperature (°C)	Zone	Temperature (°F)
–45.6 and Below	1	Below –50
–45.5 to –40.0	2	–50 to –40
–40.0 to –34.5	3	–40 to –30
–34.4 to –28.9	4	–30 to –20
–28.8 to –23.4	5	–20 to –10
–23.3 to –17.8	6	–10 to 0
–17.7 to –12.3	7	0 to 10
–12.2 to –6.7	8	10 to 20
–6.6 to –1.2	9	20 to 30
–1.1 to 4.4	10	30 to 40
4.5 and Above	11	40 and Above

200   400 km

design: D. Schreiber
courtesy of Verlag Eugen Ulmer

NURSERY SOURCES

This is a partial list of nurseries that specialize in clematis and sell plants by retail or mail-order. Catalogues or plant lists are available from most. No endorsement is intended, nor is criticism implied of sources not mentioned.

Australia

Carole's Garden Clematis Nursery
94 Bungower Road
Somerville, Victoria 3912
61 (03) 5977 9277
http://www.clematisnursery.com.au

Clematis Cottage Nursery
41 Main Street
Sheffield, Tasmania 7306
61 (03) 6491 2183
http://www.clematiscottage.com.au

Canada

Gardenimport
135 West Beaver Creek Road
Richmond Hill, Ontario L4B 1C6
1 (905) 731 1950
http://www.gardenimport.com

Mason Hogue Gardens
3520 Durham Road #1, RR#4
Uxbridge, Ontario L9P 1R4
1 (905) 649 3532
http://www.masonhogue.com

Denmark

Fleming Hansen
Solbakken 22
Ugelbølle, 8410 Rønde
45 8637 2843
http://www.clematisdanmark.dk

Estonia

Family Kivistik
Roogoja Talu
Karla Küla, Kose 75101
Harjumaa
372 603 6418

Finland

Puutarhakeskus Sofianlehto
Sofianlehdonkatu 12
00610 Helsinki
358 09 796 230
http://www.sofianlehto.com

France

Le Jardin des Clématites
5 bis allée du Fond du Val
BP 172
76135 Mont Saint Aignan
33 (0) 2 35 70 39 39

Germany

Wilhelm Kruse
Wallenbrückerstrasse 14
49328 Melle 7
49 (0) 5226 989866

Friedrich Manfred Westphal
Peiner Hof 7
D-25497 Prisdorf
49 (0) 4101 74104
http://www.clematis-westphal.de

Ireland

Mackey's Garden Centre
Castlepark Road
Sandycove, County Dublin
353 1 280 7385
www.mackeys.ie

Murphy & Wood Garden Centre
Johnstown Road
Dun Laoghaire, County Dublin
353 1 285 4855

Japan

Chikuma Nursery
1-19-27 Sugao
Miyamae-ku
Kawasaki City, Kanagawa Prefecture 216-0015
81 (0) 449 77 1187

Kasugai Engei
1709-120 Kakino Tsurusato Machi
Toki City, Gifu Prefecture 509-5312
81 (0) 572 52 2238

Shonan Clematis Nursery
3-7-24 Tsuzido-Motomachi
Fujisawa City, Kanagawa Prefecture 247-0043
81 (0) 466 36 4635
http://www.shonan-clematis.co.jp

Netherlands

Henk J. M. Kuijf
Mennonietenbuurt 116A
1427 BC, Uithoorn
31 297 568564

Rein and Mark Bulk
Rijneveld 115
2771 XV, Boskoop
31 172 212005
http:// www.hkolster.nl

New Zealand

Cadsonbury Plant Breeders
28 Vardon Crescent
Christchurch 8006
64 3 385 3475

Yaku Nursery
278 Tikorangi Road, RD 43
Waitara 4656, Taranaki
64 (0) 6 754 4500
http:// www.vanplant.co.nz/yaku/

Poland

Szkolka Pojemnikowa
ul. Duchnicka 27
05-800 Pruszków
48 22 722 2664
http://www.clematis.com.pl

Sweden

Cedergren & Co. Plantskola
Box 160 16
S 250 16 Råå
46 042 260 052
http:// www.cedergrens.com

Switzerland

Lehmann Baumschulen AG
CH-3294 Büren an der Aare
41 (0) 32 351 1519
www.lehmann-baumschulen.ch

United Kingdom

Baronscourt Nurseries
Baronscourt Road
Newtownstewart
Omagh, County Tyrone
Northern Ireland
44 (0) 28 8166 1683
www.barons-court.com

Beamish Clematis Nursery
Burntwood Cottage
Stoney Lane
Beamish, County Durham DH9 OSJ
England
44 (0) 19 1370 0202
http://www.beamishclematisnursery.co.uk

Busheyfields Nursery
Herne, Herne Bay
Kent CT6 7LJ
England
44 (0) 12 2737 5415

Caddicks Clematis Nursery
Lymm Road
Thelwall
Warrington, Cheshire WA4 2TG
England
44 (0) 19 2575 7196
http://www.caddicks-clematis.co.uk

Robin Savill
The Garden Company
Mayes Lane
Sandon
Chelmsford, Essex CM2 7RW
England
44 (0) 79 4111 5633

County Clematis
31 Sefton Lane
Maghull, Merseyside L31 8AE
England
44 (0) 15 1520 3310

Crûg Farm Plants
Griffith's Crossing
Caernarfon, Gwynedd LL55 1TU
Wales
44 (0) 12 4867 0232
http://www.crug-farm.co.uk

Floyd's Climbers and Clematis
Floyd's Farm
Bath Road
Kelston, Bath BA1 9AN
England
44 (0) 11 7967 3151

Ford Nursery
Broom Lane
Oake
Taunton, Somerset TA4 1BE
England
44 (0) 18 2346 1961

Hillmount Nursery Centre
56-58 Upper Braniel Road
Gilnahirk, Belfast BT5 7TX
Northern Ireland
44 (0) 28 9044 8213
http:// www.hillmount.co.uk

Hollybrook Nursery
Exmouth Road
West Hill
Ottery St. Mary, Devon EX11 1JZ
England
44 (0) 14 0482 2958

Lincoln Green Clematis Nursery
Sand Lane
Osgodby
Market Rasen, Lincolnshire LN8 3TE
England
44 (0) 16 7382 8222
http://www.lincsclematis.co.uk

Marcus Dancer Plants
'Kilcreggan'
Alderholt Road, Sandleheath
Fordingbridge, Hampshire SP6 1PT
England
44 (0) 142 5652 7470

Paddocks Nursery
Sutton
Tenbury Wells, Worcestershire WR15 8RJ
England
44 (0) 15 8481 9558

Priorswood Clematis Nursery
Priorswood, Widbury Hill
Ware, Hertfordshire SG12 7QH
England
44 (0) 19 2046 1543
http://www.priorswoodclematis.co.uk

Roseland House Nursery
Roseland House
Chacewater
Truro, Cornwall TR4 8QB
England
44 (0) 18 7256 0451
http://www.roselandhouse.co.uk

Redheads Clematis
Greenacres Nursery
Eastwood End, Wimblington
March, Cambridgeshire PE15 0QQ
England
44 (0) 13 5474 0501
http://www.redheads-clematis.co.uk

Sheila Chapman Clematis
At Crowther Nurseries
Ongar Road
Abridge, Essex RM4 1AA
England
44 (0) 17 0868 8090
http://www.sheilachapman.co.uk

Taylor's Clematis
Sutton Road
Sutton, Askern
Doncaster, South Yorkshire DN6 9JZ
England
44 (0) 13 0270 0716
http://www.taylorsclematis.co.uk

Thorncroft Clematis Nursery
The Lings
Reymerston
Norwich, Norfolk NR9 4QG
England
44 (0) 19 5385 0407
http://www.thorncroft.co.uk

Woodcote Park Nursery
Ripley Road
Send
Woking, Surrey GU23 7LT
England
44 (0) 14 8322 3623

United States

Chalk Hill Clematis Farm
11720 Chalk Hill Road
Healdsburg, California 95448
(707) 433-8416
http://www.chalkhillclematis.com

Collector's Nursery
16804 NE 102nd Avenue
Battle Ground, Washington 98604
(360) 574-3832
http://www.collectorsnursery.com

Completely Clematis Speciality Nursery
217 Argilla Road
Ipswich, Massachusetts 01938
(978) 356-3197
http://www.clematisnursery.com

Donahue's Clematis Specialists
420 SW 10th Street
Faribault, Minnesota 55021
(507) 334-8404
http://www.donahuesgreenhouse.com

Heronswood Nursery
7530 NE 288th Street
Kingston, Washington 98346
(360) 297-4172
http:// www.heronswood.com

Joy Creek Nursery
20300 NW Watson Road
Scappoose, Oregon 97056
(503) 543-7474
http://www.joycreek.com

Siskiyou Rare Plant Nursery
2825 Cummings Road
Medford, Oregon 97501
(541) 772-6846
http://www.siskiyourareplantnursery.com

Wayside Gardens
1 Garden Lane
Hodges, South Carolina 29695
(800) 213-0379
http://www.waysidegardens.com

GLOSSARY

achene a small dry fruit enclosing a single seed and not splitting to scatter the seed. In *Clematis*, a collection of achenes is called a seedhead.

axil the angle between a leaf and the stem of a plant where the axillary bud develops.

cultivar a cultivated variety, a plant originating under cultivation.

foliage a collective term for the leaves of a plant.

hard prune to cut back the aboveground shoots on a plant to within a few buds from the base. This type of pruning promotes vigorous growth.

herbaceous a term used to describe the habit of plants, mostly perennials, which die down at the end of a growing season and return to full growth above ground level the following spring.

humus a rich brownish black material resulting from the gradual breakdown of vegetable and other organic matter by bacterial activity.

hybrid a plant obtained by the crossing of two different varieties, species, or genera of plants. Hybrids seldom breed true and some are even sterile.

internode the part of the stem between two consecutive nodes (leaf joints).

node a point where the leaf is attached to the stem, also known as the leaf joint.

pendulous hanging, drooping, or suspended (of a flower).

persistent not dropping or falling off, as in the case of the feathery style of a clematis seed (achene).

petaloid petal-like. Sepals and staminodes, or sterile stamens, can look like petals.

pH the measure of acidity or alkalinity of any substance.

recurved curved backward or downward (of tepals).

reflexed fully bent or turned back on itself (the tip of a tepal, for example).

scandent climbing unassisted by tendrils or other modified structures.

sepal a component of the calyx, the outermost whorl of flower. Sepals are usually green and leaf-like. Sometimes they may become brightly colored like the petals or even replace the petals, as is the case in *Clematis*.

solitary a term used to describe flowers when they appear singly rather than in clusters.

species a basic unit of biological classification which refers to a group of very closely related plants which can interbreed freely and breed true with one another but not usually with members of another species. If they do, the resulting hybrids will be infertile.

stamen the male reproductive part of a flower made up of a filament and anther.

staminode an infertile stamen, a stamen with no pollen.

subshrub a shrublike plant in which only the basal part becomes woody.

subspecies a subdivision of a species, consisting of a plant which usually differs in two or more characteristics from the typical plant and is geographically distinct.

synonym an alternate name or an earlier name that has been replaced.

temperate mild, often used to describe climate.

tepal a term used when there is no clear differentiation between a sepal (calyx) and a petal (corolla), as is the case with *Clematis*.

terminal at the very end of a stem or shoot, ending it.

× a sign used for hybridization.

FURTHER READING

Beutler, L. 2004. *Gardening with Clematis: Design and Cultivation*. Timber Press.

Chesshire, C. 2004. *Clematis: Inspiration, Selection, and Practical Guidance*. Quadrille Publishing.

Evison, R. J. 2003. *The Gardener's Guide to Growing Clematis*. Timber Press.

Fretwell, B. 1994. *Clematis as Companion Plants*. Collins.

Fretwell, B. 1999. *A Comprehensive Guide*. HarperCollins.

Gooch, R. 1996. *Clematis: The Complete Guide*. Crowood Press.

Howells, J. 1996. *The Rose and the Clematis as Good Companions*. Garden Art Press.

Howells, J. 1998. *Trouble-free Clematis: The Viticellas*. Garden Art Press.

Toomey, M. 1999. *Clematis: A Care Manual*. Hamlyn Publishers.

Toomey, M., E. Leeds, and C. Cheshire. 2001. *An Illustrated Encyclopedia of Clematis*. Timber Press.

INDEX

ABOUT THE AUTHORS

Mary Toomey, M.SC., PH.D., trained as a biologist, botanist, entomologist, and soil ecologist. She has been growing and studying clematis for more than 30 years. A former editor of the British Clematis Society journal, *The Clematis*, she is the founder and chairman of the Ranunculaceae Society. Mary is well known as a broadcaster, international lecturer on clematis and gardening, and author of articles for horticultural journals and several college textbooks on biology. She designed the Clematis Display garden in Chalkhill Clematis Nursery in Healdsburg, California. Born in Jaffna, Sri Lanka, Mary currently lives and gardens in Dublin, Ireland.

Photo by Carol Leeds.

Everett Leeds is a founding member of the International Clematis Society and the British Clematis Society, and a former chairman of the latter. For more than 30 years he has been growing and breeding small-flowered clematis in his large garden in Surrey, England. He contributes regularly to *The Clematis*.

Photo by Anne de Charmant.

Charles Chesshire is a garden designer, lecturer, and writer. He has designed gardens in the United States, France, and Britain. Charles is consultant to Sudeley Castle Gardens in Gloucestershire, United Kingdom, and was curator to the National Collection of Clematis held in Burford House Gardens, Worcestershire, for a number of years. He has published several books on clematis and other gardening topics, and has been a regular contributor to *The Sunday Times*.